THE OLDEST KITCHEN IN THE WORLD

4,000 YEARS OF MIDDLE EASTERN COOKING PASSED DOWN THROUGH GENERATIONS

MATAY DE MAYEE

THE OLDEST KITCHEN IN THE WORLD

4,000 YEARS
OF MIDDLE EASTERN COOKING
PASSED DOWN THROUGH
GENERATIONS

T tra.publishing

This cookbook fills a long-existing void in culinary literature. Surprisingly, no specific cookbook exists for what is arguably the oldest cuisine in the world. The recipes of the Assyrians—Christians from the Middle East, also known as Syriacs, Chaldeans, or Arameans—have been passed down from mother to daughter for centuries without a cookbook or written notes. My six siblings and I barely know how to prepare my mother's dishes, a fact I have often wondered about. Perhaps we had too many distractions outside the house during our youth. Or perhaps one naturally becomes a little lazy when growing up with a mother who cooks so deliciously. Regardless, all these exquisite flavors and textures should not be lost. It's high time to learn to cook from the world's best Assyrian chef: my mother. She is essentially the author of this cookbook; however, there's one small problem—my mother grew up in a place and time when girls didn't learn to read or write. Therefore, I am writing it on her behalf.

———— Matay de Mayee

Table of Contents

- 8   A Note from the Author
- 12   The Assyrians
- 14   In the Assyrian Kitchen
- 18   Special Days on the Calendar
- 22   A Few Words About the Language
- 24   Getting Started
- 26   My Mother's Kitchen Shelf
- 30   Grains
- 33   Childhood Memories
- 35   At the Table
- 36   Kolonya

Recipes

- 38   Kul naqa- *Always on the Table*
- 60   A klasikoye- *The Classics*
- 93   Busholé u mukloné mbashlé- *Soups and Stews*
- 115   Yarqunwotho, yariqutho u sharko- *Vegetables and More*
- 151   Baṣroné u nuné- *Meat and Fish*
- 183   Ḥalyutho- *Divine Sweets*

- 214   Acknowledgments
- 217   Index

A Note from the Author

No Assyrian household is complete without a well-stocked pantry and an even more abundant table. I love visiting my mother because she always has something delicious to eat and serves it in no time. She wouldn't consider herself a good hostess otherwise. She learned this art from her mother, who wanted to ensure my mother mastered all the nuances of the Syriac-Assyrian (West-Assyrian) kitchen. My grandmother had imagined that if my mother couldn't cook, she wouldn't find a man who would want to marry her. As it turns out, my father wouldn't have minded if she could not cook, because he himself was a cook during his military service!

In the late 1960s, my parents bravely decided to start a new life in the Netherlands. They settled in the eastern city of Hengelo, where most of my siblings and I were born. Despite our Dutch upbringing, we have thankfully not lost our language and traditions. We all still speak fluent Surayt, a dialect of Aramaic. We have breakfast together at Easter and Christmas, and visit the Syriac Orthodox monastery every year—a monastery that was partially founded by my father. And of course, there's the joy of frequently relishing the traditional dishes my mother prepares.

I wrote this book to capture and preserve these dishes. Although most of the recipes don't require much time to prepare, in my memory, my mother seemed to be in the kitchen all day. This might be because she had seven growing children and always kept her house open to guests. I don't have as much time to spend in the kitchen as she did. Therefore, it remains to be seen if I can combine my desire to cook Assyrian with my busy life. I have occasionally searched for restaurants near me that cook authentic Assyrian food, but have so far come up short.

Our only choice to get a taste of home is to join my mother at her table—and rest assured, such an experience is certainly no punishment. The dining table, whether it be hers or any Assyrian family's, is the heart of our culture, a symbol of our togetherness, and the embodiment of our hospitality. All I can say now is: enjoy!

Or, in other words, HANIYÉ!

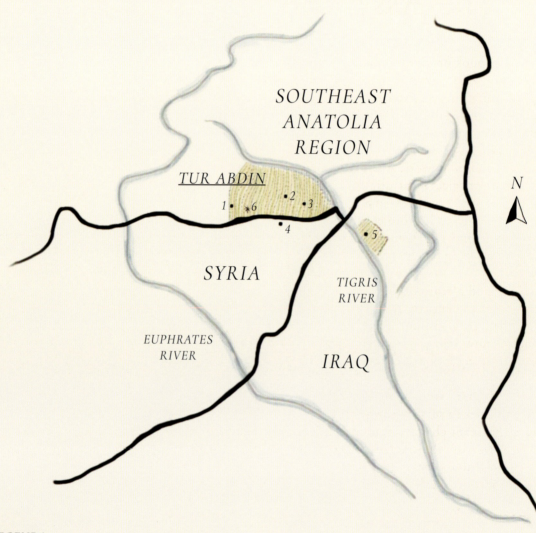

The Assyrians

This cookbook originates not in a country but in a people, the people of our family: the Assyrians, also known as Syriacs, Chaldeans, or Arameans. They once were part of the Assyrian Empire. Around 2000 BCE, this empire, along with Sumeria, Akkadia, and Babylonia, contributed to the formation of the Mesopotamian civilization. Assyrian territory encompassed the north of Mesopotamia, or parts of southeast Turkey, northern Iraq, northeast Syria, and northwest Iran—borders that are only a century old, drawn by former colonial powers. A small community still lives in the area, but most have settled in North America, Australia, and Western Europe. Regardless of where they live, the Assyrians are characterized by the same (culinary!) traditions and large families that are very close and loyal to each other. They predominantly practice Christianity, with many still speaking fluent Surayt and Suret(h), dialects of Aramaic, presumed to be the language spoken by Jesus.

The fate and history of the Assyrians, especially the horrific tragedy that unfolded in the twentieth century, are unknown to many people. During the Armenian genocide of 1915, the Ottomans murdered 1.5 million Christian Armenians. The Assyrians were not spared; more than 300,000 fell victim. We call these mass killings the Sayfo, an Aramaic word meaning "sword," because many victims were killed by the sword.

On my mother's side, in my own family's history, my grandmother and her father were the only ones to survive the genocide. To this day, Christian Assyrians continue to face significant challenges in the Middle East. The rise of ISIS, which has driven many Christians from their homes, did not make things any easier. Fortunately, the Assyrians are a resilient and persistent people and always find each other, especially at the one place where everyone can momentarily forget all their worries: the dining table.

In the Assyrian Kitchen

Roughly four thousand years ago, an Assyrian used Akkadian cuneiform (believed to be the earliest writing system) to inscribe a method for stewing and seasoning sheep or goat meat. The ancient scribe listed the required ingredients on a clay tablet and described the cooking process. Discovered alongside two other tablets in 1933, these texts comprise the world's oldest cookbook. It is not an exaggeration to say that a direct line can be traced from this clay-tablet cookbook to the Assyrian matbakh (kitchen/cuisine)—or more personally, my mother's kitchen. For clarification, here is a brief overview of the historical context:

At the time, the Assyrian Empire covered the northern part of Mesopotamia, the land between the Tigris and Euphrates rivers, called Beth Nahrin. This is where agriculture first developed, and almost immediately, the art of cooking followed. The Assyrians spoke Akkadian, which, around 1000 BCE, was gradually replaced by Aramaic, the language of the Arameans who migrated into the region during that period. Aramaic, a dialect of which my mother and I speak, adopted many words for recipes, ingredients, and techniques from ancient Akkadian. Notable examples include *kebabu*, which means "grilled or roasted," and *kamunu*, which translates to "cumin." These words predate the introduction of Arabic to these regions. The Assyrian matbakh treasures these ancient terms and, thus, forms the bedrock of all Middle Eastern cuisines, such as Turkish, Lebanese, Greek, Israeli, and Armenian. Spices like nigella seeds or Aleppo pepper are ubiquitous, and dishes like apprakhe (pg. 70) or baklava (pg. 200) are widespread.

Naturally, there are also differences in the region's culinary traditions, often due to another significant influence on the Assyrian kitchen: the advent of Christianity. Unlike Judaism or Islam, there are no restrictions on consuming pork or alcohol.

The Assyrians celebrate Easter, Christmas, and numerous other holidays, and observe many fasting periods. These religious practices significantly shape the culinary calendar. For example, fasting occurs in the spring before Easter, typically during a time of meat scarcity. Afterward, when the livestock give birth to their young, milk is abundant for making yogurt and cheese. In the summer, the hard work of harvesting crops, often under the sweltering heat, necessitates easy-to-prepare dishes like labaniyeh (pg. 83) or burghul (bulgur) (pg. 42). Various vegetables, fruits, and nuts grace the table after the autumn harvest. Later, livestock, such as sheep, cows, and goats, are slaughtered, and the meat is preserved for winter through salting. Vegetables and fruits are dried and canned. When winter sets in, and the fields lie dormant, there is more time to prepare more elaborate dishes. Kötle (pg. 80) remains a favorite, but samborakat (pg. 64) and tawa (pg. 67) are also immensely popular.

In the Assyrian kitchen, a substantial warm lunch is the main meal of the day, while breakfast and dinner tend to be lighter. Each meal is served with crispy fresh bread, preferably baked in a tanuro—the term comes from an Akkadian word (*tinuru*) that means "clay oven" (also the root of the Indian word *tandoori*). Traditionally, cooking is done on an open fire between two stones called the tfayo.

Modern Assyrian cuisine still heavily features herbs, spices, grains, vegetables, legumes, and minimal fats. Chicken and lamb are the predominant meats, with beef also being a common choice. Pork is less prevalent, primarily due to its scarcity in regions predominantly inhabited by Muslims in the Middle East. Fish is also rarely on the menu due to its short shelf life in the warm climate, and because many Assyrian people live far from the sea or large rivers. Nevertheless, this book includes a few beautiful fish recipes.

Now we'll delve deeper into the culinary traditions of the Syriac-Assyrian (West-Assyrian) kitchen.

Special Days on the Calendar

Celebration days for the Assyrians revolve around food—whether it's consumed in abundance, the diet is shifting due to the seasons, or it's a time of fasting. Special dishes are sometimes prepared, primarily based on religious observances such as Easter, Christmas, or the period following a fast. Great effort goes into these special meals. Weddings and funerals also have specific dishes on the menu. However, the way these feast days and memorial days are celebrated is changing, which isn't surprising because most Assyrians have emigrated and spread across the globe. In regions where larger communities still live together, traditions are predominantly upheld in family gatherings and churches, albeit often in modified forms. Nonetheless, in this book, my mother and I have strived to maintain the culinary calendar in its most original form. Here's an overview of the special days on the calendar, starting with fasting periods.

Saumo (Fasting Period)

During a fasting period (known as saumo), consuming food of animal origin, such as meat, milk, or eggs, is forbidden. Fish is an exception and is allowed, serving as a substitute for meat. Olive oil, sunflower oil, or margarine is used instead of butter. Because of this tradition, we have many vegetarian dishes, with vegetables, grains, and legumes playing a significant role.

There are two lengthy saumo periods: fifty days before Easter (Saumo rabo) and ten days before Christmas (Saumo z'uro). Popular dishes during these times include tlawhé (pg. 96), hemse (pg. 100), matfuniye doe farmo (pg. 113), and ballo' (pg. 146). There is also a three-day fasting period called Saumo d'Ninwe, which requires total abstinence from food and drink (except for water); it is named after the ancient city of Ninive, now known as Mosul, on the Tigris River in Iraq. During these fasting days, people remember the story of Jonah. A large fish swallowed him, and he ended up alive but stuck in the belly of the beast. At God's command, the fish expelled Jonah after three days, and this intervention prevented the impending destruction of Ninive. Observing the Saumo Ninive is challenging. After the fast, the first thing people eat is a cake called qawité (pg. 208).

Hano Qritho (Carnival)

Enduring fifty days of restricted eating before celebrating Easter is no small feat. No wonder everyone wants to eat and drink exuberantly beforehand. This indulgence happens during Hano Qritho, our version of the Carnival festive season, on the last Sunday before the fast period begins. *Hano Qritho* translates to "village girl." The "village girl" symbolizes fertility, spring, and the upcoming harvest. An old custom involves making a doll representing a girl and filling it with candies. At the end of the day, children are allowed to break the doll and share the sweets. But before that happens, they go door to door to collect bulgur, eggs, and meat. To this day, traditional Assyrians gather in the church on this occasion, where bulgur with scrambled eggs and qaliyo (pickled meat) is shared.

Suboro (Announcement)

On March 25, exactly nine months before Christmas, the Assyrians celebrate the announcement of Christ's birth with Suboro, which in our language means "announcement" (of the birth of Christ to Mary). We braid strands of white and red wool and distribute them in the church. White represents the divine, and red signifies humanity. These strings, known as suboro, can be worn around the fingers, on the wrist, or as earrings. They are only removed on Easter Monday. During Suboro, people also bake unleavened bread, and ideally have it blessed by a priest.

Hedo Rabo (Easter)

Easter is the most significant and oldest celebration for the Assyrian people. Some families, including mine, still follow the Julian calendar, so our Easter celebrations sometimes occur later than those in Gregorian-calendar churches. We celebrate the first day of Easter with family and friends, and the second day is dedicated to commemorating the deceased. It is a day of remembering loved ones and visiting their burial sites. Naturally, good food and drink are integral. For my mother, this is the busiest time of the year. She makes everything herself, from yogurt (pg. 45) and cheese (pg. 52) to braided soft sweet rolls (pg. 196) and cookies (pg. 199). And of course, there are eggs. We don't paint the eggs but rather give them a red color by boiling them with onion skins (pg. 136).

Hewolo (Marriage)

If there's a moment when the Assyrian celebrate extravagantly, it is at a wedding. After the marriage ceremony, there's abundant eating, drinking, singing, and dancing. Row and circle dances, which have their origins in the joyful jumps performed during grain harvests, are especially popular. Guests line up in circles, forming one large loop or several smaller ones. They don't hold hands; instead, they connect pinky to pinky in a dance familiar to every Assyrian. Those who wish can sit for a while and enjoy special dishes like dobo (pg. 106) or fasuliye (pgs. 110 and 149). The day after the wedding, the bride and groom, now called *sabahiye* ("newlyweds"), traditionally eat samborakat (pg. 64) for breakfast.

Ufoyo (Funeral)

When an Assyrian dies, the news is communicated by word of mouth amongst the community. Ample time is taken for mourning. Before the funeral, condolence meetings are held in the church for three days. These meetings feature improvised songs about the deceased, sung by the eldest women to offer comfort. During the meetings, food isn't forgotten. Stews with lamb, beef, or fish and rolls are served. Traditionally, no alcohol is available: only black coffee and tea, without sugar. The bitter taste symbolizes sorrow. Forty days after the death, when the mourning period concludes, people traditionally eat homemade bread or dashisto (pg. 204).

A Few Words About the Language

It is through Aramaic, the language that replaced Akkadian, both in Mesopotamia and as a lingua franca in the wider Near East, that the vast majority of the Akkadian linguistic legacy has been transmitted. It is not surprising that such influence is found especially in the Mesopotamian dialects of Aramaic, that is, the forms of Aramaic that were in immediate contact with spoken Akkadian during its final centuries of use.

(*History of the Akkadian Language*, Volume VIII, *Afterlife: Akkadian after Akkadian*, Chapter 26, "The Legacy of Akkadian," Paragraph 4, Akkadian in Aramaic, pg. 1489)

I have chosen to label all dishes in this book with their original Aramaic names, along with a translation or description. The term *Aramaic*, however, is only partially accurate, as the Assyrians today speak dialects of it: namely Surayt (Central Aramaic) and Suret(h) (Eastern Aramaic). Around the eighteenth century BCE, Assyrians in Mesopotamia inscribed the world's oldest known culinary recipes on tablets using cuneiform. These recipes were written in Akkadian, the language of the Assyrian Empire. However, demographic shifts around 1000 BCE led to the introduction of Aramaic into Assyria. Aramaic gained official status shortly after and gradually replaced the native Akkadian language.

Despite this linguistic shift, the languages Surayt and Suret(h) still contain numerous Akkadian words, illustrating their connection to Mesopotamian heritage. I have included a list of several significant words in the glossary, as understanding them provides deeper insight into the culinary heritage discussed in this book.

Examples of Contemporary Dialects that Have Their Origins in Akkadian

Surayt - Turoyo	Suret(h) - Assyrian	Akkadian
adro - threshing floor	edra - threshing floor	adru - threshing floor
muklo / ukholo - food	ekhala - food	akalu - eat/food
'ezo - goat	ezza - goat	enzu - goat
s'oré - barley	saré - barley	še'u - barley
raymuno / armunto - pomegranate	armunta - pomegranate	armannu - pomegranate
semdo - semolina flour	smida - semolina flour	samidu - fine flour or semolina
yarqutho - vegetables	yarquta - vegetables	arqu - vegetables
ro'yo - shepherd	raya - shepherd	rā'iu - shepherd
ṣaydo - hunting	ṣayda - hunting	ṣâdu - hunting
kabab - kebab	kabab - kebab	kababu - kebab
qarsyo - cherry	qarsya - cherry	girīṣu - cherry
tumo - garlic	tuma - garlic	šūmu - garlic
busholo - to cook	bushala - to cook	bašalu - to cook
kamuno - cumin	kamuna - cumin	kamûnu - cumin
kisbartho - coriander	kisbarta - coriander	kisibirrītu - coriander
kurkmo - turmeric*	kurkama - turmeric	kurkanu - turmeric
emro - lamb	emra - lamb	emmeru - lamb
zaro'utho - farming/agriculture	zruta - farming/agriculture	zarûtu - farming/agriculture
qamḥo - flour	qimkha - flour	qēmu - flour
nin'o - mint	ninna - mint	naniḫu - mint
hṣodo - harvest	khṣada - harvest	esādu - harvest
tanuro - oven	tanura - oven	tinuru - oven
kantro - pear	kamotra - pear	kamešševu - pear
khawkho - peach	khokha - peach	ḫaḫḫu - peach
karoto - leek	karata - leek	karašu - leek
za'faran - saffron	zapiran - saffron	azupiranu - saffron
sheshmo - sesame	sheshma - sesame	šamšamu - sesame
ḥassé - lettuce	khassé - lettuce	ḫassū - lettuce
ṣatro - thyme	ṣatra - thyme	ṣataru - thyme
shemko - onion**	shemkha - onion	šumku - onion
ten(t)o - fig	ten(t)a - fig	tittu - fig
nunto - fish	nunta - fish	nūnu - fish
basro - meat	bisra - meat	šīru - meat
karmo - vineyard	karma - vineyard	karmu - vineyard

* *Kurkmo* can mean both "saffron" and "turmeric."
** However, the more commonly used words are *baslo / bisla*.

Getting Started

I've long envisioned this cookbook, though, as noted in the introduction, its true origin is in my mother's mind. She carried all the recipes from her homeland, recipes that were handed down orally from mother to daughter for generations. Nowhere was anything documented. Nothing was measured. Everything was done by intuition. My task was to convert those pinches, dashes, and bits into precise, comprehensible recipes, and to standardize the slicing, chopping, stirring, folding, kneading, and tasting involved.

My mother preserved the original names of the dishes as much as possible, and I translated them. We know the dishes by the same names, but they are prepared differently in each kitchen. This variation partially stems from the Assyrian diaspora. From Sweden to Australia, India to the United States, the Assyrians have established themselves globally. My mother's kitchen has its unique accents, but she endeavored to maintain the recipes' authenticity. Any Assyrian would instantly recognize the dishes' taste, aroma, and texture.

Feel free to taste and adjust the dishes according to your palate. If the outcome is disappointing the first time, don't hesitate to try again. My mother taught me traditional cooking, and it is always remarkable when she tastes my cooking and a smile appears on her face. If the taste is off, she immediately tells me what is missing. She is not easily satisfied.

We didn't choose the recipes in this book randomly. In making our selection, my mother and I deemed it important that the dishes included here be those that continue to be loved and often prepared by the Assyrians. And, perhaps most crucially, we find them delicious ourselves.

All dishes share one thing in common. They are best when prepared with fresh ingredients. We recommend you shop at local Middle Eastern or Turkish stores whenever possible—a visit can be delightful, and can inspire new ideas. I'm always surprised by the range, the price, and especially the quality of food available. The vegetables, for example, often contain less water and are smaller; however, they are much more flavorful. Most items don't have plastic packaging because nearly everything is fresh. But if you are having difficulty sourcing ingredients, most are now available online.

The Assyrian cuisine reflects the countryside: it's honest and unpretentious. It focuses on authentic recipes that are not overly complicated. The dishes remind me of comfort food and always evoke a warm feeling. A stew simmering all day on the stove, spreading delightful, mouthwatering aromas throughout the house, always brings back memories of family gatherings and makes the indoors feel cozy and inviting. Nothing could make me happier.

My Mother's Kitchen Shelf

When I was doing my homework in the attic room of my youth, I could always know my mother was cooking by the delicious smells wafting up daily. I could often identify the dish being prepared by its aroma, and if not, I could at least discern which spices she used, as they were unmistakable. She had everything within reach: herbs, spices, grains—all on her kitchen shelf, ingredients in every Assyrian kitchen. Most are used daily, but there are also very specific ones used for special dishes like Easter bread. Luckily, all these ingredients have a long shelf life and are readily available. Most ingredients, such as parsley or tomato paste, are self-explanatory; others require further clarification. Here is a description of the key ingredients included in the following recipes.

Aleppo Pepper

Coarsely ground dried red pepper. Originally from Aleppo in Syria, one of the oldest cities in the world. The flavor is spicy yet mild and sweet (the spicy seeds have been removed). Highly loved in the Middle East, Aleppo pepper is often used in both warm and cold dishes and is a staple on the table.

Dried Mint

Crushed dried leaves of green mint. It has a more pungent taste than fresh mint and is used for salads and warm dishes.

Grape Molasses

Reduced juice from pressed grapes. It is syrupy, with a dark brown color and a caramelized taste. It is used primarily in sweet dishes and as a topping for flatbreads. Opt for the version without added sugar.

Mahlab

Mahlab is a spice derived from the seed of the pit of the sour cherry tree, a species native to the Middle East, among other places. The seed is ground into a fine powder, yielding a flavor reminiscent of bitter almonds. It's a popular flavor enhancer in dishes like sweet rolls and cookies.

Mastic

Mastic is a spice comprised of transparent yellow grains made from the dried resin of the mastic tree. It has a unique pine-like flavor and is used as a flavoring for festive breads. If you have difficulty finding it, a good substitute is vanilla.

Nigella Seed

Nigella seed is a spice from the black seed of the *Nigella sativa* plant, which grows in Syria, Turkey, and Iraq. Its taste is somewhat nutty and peppery, and it is predominantly used in baking bread or cookies. Despite some references, it is not related to black cumin or black sesame seed.

Pomegranate Molasses

Thick syrup from reduced pomegranate juice with a sweet-sour taste. Dark red and mainly used for savory dishes. It should not be confused with the syrup used in pomegranate lemonade.

Seven-Spice Powder

This is a blend of seven equal parts of finely ground spices like coriander, cloves, cinnamon, nutmeg, allspice, pepper, and cumin. It is primarily used in meat dishes, and there are various blends. The powder is easy to make at home, but the store-bought versions also maintain high quality.

Sumac

Sumac is a spice made from the sumac plant's dried and coarsely ground red berries. It has a tangy lemon-like flavor and is used in hot and cold savory dishes.

Turkish Green Pepper

The long, slender Turkish green pepper, larger than the Spanish variety, comes in shades of light or dark green. It is often eaten raw with meals but can also be cooked or grilled. The light green variety resembles a pointed bell pepper and is less spicy than the dark green variety.

Grains

About ten thousand years ago, hunter-gatherers in the fertile land between the Euphrates and the Tigris rivers had the idea of planting a seed to grow nutrient-rich grass. That plant was wheat. Excavations show that wheat grains were already being hulled, crushed, ground, and cooked in ancient times. The oldest recipes in our cuisine primarily use durum, a hard wheat variety. It is the basis, the starting point in the kitchen of Assyrians.

My mother sometimes recounts, with a hint of distaste, how when she was a young girl, cows would thresh the wheat by walking over the freshly cut grain. This method was as simple as it was effective. The kernels would fall out of the ears and stalks and then be processed and prepared in numerous dishes.

My mother can hardly imagine it now, but when she was young, she ground grain by hand! She used two small millstones, one equipped with two wooden handles. She would rotate one stone over the other, grinding the grain sandwiched between them. Grinding grain was too heavy a task to undertake alone, so she did it with her younger sister.

The oldest recipes in our cuisine primarily use durum, a hard wheat variety. In North Africa, durum is used to make couscous, and in Italy, pasta—but we mainly use it for bulgur. The kernels are first boiled, then dried outdoors on flat roofs, and only then ground. While we don't bake bread from bulgur, it lends itself to the most delicious dishes.

Nowadays, the process is different. Store-bought bulgur is oven dried, mechanically ground, and varies from a very fine to a very coarse grind because different recipes call for bulgur of varying coarseness. As a rule of thumb, fine-ground and extra-fine-ground bulgur, which we call hurek, are used in salads and in cold and hot dishes. The medium, coarse, and extra-coarse grinds are usually eaten as a side dish like rice or potatoes.

Below is a list of some of the dishes made from different grinds. This includes some made from other common wheat products in Assyrian cuisine, such as semolina, hulled wheat kernels, raw gruel, and vermicelli, supplemented with rice and barley grains. These grains are available at Middle Eastern supermarkets, Turkish grocers, natural food stores, or online retailers.

- *Extra-fine and fine**
Acin (extra-fine)
Kötle (extra-fine)
Kibbeh saniye (extra-fine)
Ballo' (fine)
Itj (fine)
Tabouleh (fine)

- *Medium, coarse, and extra-coarse**
Side dishes (often cooked with rice)

- *Semolina from hard wheat*
Harise (sweet cake)

- *Hulled wheat (gheetee)*
Labaniyeh

- *Wheat groats / uncooked broken wheat (gerso)*
Kötle (fine)
Gerso (coarse)
Gabula (coarse)

- *Vermicelli (sh'iraye)*
Often fried in butter, then cooked with bulgur or rice

- *Rice, usually long-grain or basmati, except for the following, which use short-grain rice, such as for risotto:*
Apprakhe
Fulful hashyo
Dashisto
Maqloubeh
Tlawhé
M'wothé

- *Barley (schoree)*
Raw material for beer and animal feed

* In the Middle Eastern supermarket, the bulgur grinds are often called *köftelik* ("fine"), *midyat* ("medium"), *pilavlik* ("coarse"), and *iri pilavlik* ("extra-coarse").

Childhood Memories

My mother often reminisces about her carefree youth. She grew up in a small village in the countryside with a home garden and free-roaming animals. There was no refrigerator and no electricity. She vividly recalls the delicious taste of everything back then, especially when it was grown on my grandparents' land. By comparison, she often finds that today's produce lacks flavor. She also believes that we are now too quick to store things in the refrigerator (when it's not necessary), and it often negatively alters the taste. Condiments such as store-bought mayonnaise or ketchup didn't exist when she was young; neither did baby food from a jar. Everything was homemade.

Cooking was done using pots set on stones with a fire (tfayo, a traditional open-fire cooking method). Fresh bread was baked daily in a tanuro (or traditional oven with heat-retentive clay walls), and meat dishes were prepared in a ground oven (known as pit cooking) where the fire was underground and cooked without a timer or thermometer. Using three methods was helpful for preparing a large amount of food simultaneously. And it all happened outdoors, under all weather conditions, even in the snow!

My grandparents grew everything themselves and lived off their harvest. Their diet mainly consisted of grains, especially wheat and barley. Wheat was seen as a luxury product, while barley was primarily cultivated as animal feed or as a raw material for beer. They also grew legumes, such as lentils, chickpeas, and beans, which are staple foods in the Middle East. Hummus, a puree of chickpeas and tahini, was and still is a favorite side dish. They also grew onions, garlic, bell peppers, cucumbers, cabbages, lettuce, and melons on their land. Fruits such as figs, pomegranates, and apricots flourished on trees in abundance. There were herbs like coriander, parsley, and mint. Butter and cheese were made from sheep's, goat's, and cow's milk. Meat was not consumed daily; it was a luxury. Cattle were primarily used for heavy work in the fields. When beef was used, it served as stuffing for dishes. Chicken was eaten all year round. In the absence of pigs, wild boars were hunted for meat. The sheep was by far the most favored for its meat, whether lambs or adult animals, fat or lean, from the plains or the mountains.

My family also had a vineyard and produced wine, grape molasses, raisins, and other delicacies such as 'oliqé. The grape leaves were eaten as well, filled with a seasoned minced meat mixture.

An amusing story from my mother is that her family also "grew" chewing gum. Store-bought chewing gum did not exist back then, but they had a mastic tree, and the natural resin extracted from it was used as chewing gum. The appeal was not so much in the somewhat pine-like taste, but rather in the enjoyment they got from chewing.

At the Table

When I was a child, the doorbell rang often—an aunt, an uncle, cousins, or dear friends dropped by frequently. And, of course, everyone stayed for a meal. Only later did I come to understand that my mother seamlessly prepared a full meal for at least five extra unexpected people with the help of our chest freezer, which was always brimming with dishes she'd prepared ahead of time. After all, she often cooked too much, so the leftovers were frozen. And, of course, our pantry was stocked with grains, olives, pickled vegetables, and more. My mother welcomed each and every visitor with kolonya (pg. 36) and bonbons on a silver tray. After a warm greeting of hugs and kisses, my father would invite everyone to the table. Then, several unspoken rules applied. The guests were prioritized and took their seats at the table first. Then came my father, followed by the older children and then the younger ones. My mother served the food. If there was not enough room—and there was never enough room with seven children—we were expected to wait our turn patiently. This often meant eating in a second shift, which usually included my mother.

We did not serve appetizers or desserts. The pots were simply placed on the table, and you served yourself until full. My mother, however, encouraged guests to eat more. *Agoeloe! Agoeloe!* she would say, which means "Eat! Eat!" Out of politeness, the guests would decline several times, only to eventually give in. Moderation is not a priority at the Assyrian table.

During the meal, we shared memories, primarily about the homeland, the Assyrians still living in Northeast Syria, Southeast Turkey, Iraq, and Lebanon, and their hope for a better future there.

My parents belong to the first generation of Assyrians who settled outside their homeland, and the countless anecdotes and stories made for long and pleasant meals. When the pot was almost empty, my father always said, "You take the last bite, then it tastes better for me," which has always stayed with me.

After the meal, guests typically thanked the host with the words *sufra dayme* ("may your table always be filled"), and then everyone moved to the living room. There, as in almost all Assyrian households, a plate of fresh and dried fruits was served along with black tea (chayé).

The evening continued with a round of Assyrian digestifs. Then, whiskey, liqueur, raki (a distilled grape alcohol), and beer were brought to the table, accompanied by pistachios, walnuts, and more delectable treats. Nibbling on bozar'é (salted white pumpkin seeds) was traditional and required a special technique that every Assyrian mastered. Guests would break the seed between their incisors, releasing the flavorful kernel inside. This was a favorite pastime that often lasted the whole evening. No dish, tray, or glass remained empty for long because my mother meticulously kept everything refilled. As a result, guests often lingered, and before you knew it, another day would find them back at our door, which was always open for returning guests.

Kolonya

When I pass by a drugstore or a perfume shop, I can't resist stepping inside to smell old-fashioned 4711 Eau de Cologne. Instantly, I'm back in my parents' home, where the delightful aroma of "kolonya," our version of eau de cologne, lingered. It had the well-known lemon scent and notes of orange, bergamot, lavender, or rose. Kolonya plays a significant part in social rituals in the Middle East, especially among the Assyrians. Kolonya is typically decanted into beautifully decorated glassware and, if possible, is given a prominent place in the living room. This was also the case with my mother, who wanted her guests to have everything they needed. A dinner or party would always begin with guests being offered kolonya to refresh their hands and faces. This practice is similar to providing wet towels before meals in the Far East. Beyond its hygienic purposes, kolonya is also offered in the Middle East as a gesture of hospitality and politeness. Scent brings back more memories than any other sensory experience. The scents of my mother's dishes evoke memories, but especially evocative was the aroma of "her" kolonya!

KUL NAQA

―――― Always on the Table

Bulgur - Tomato - White Onion - Rice - Olive Oil - Dill - Cilantro - Thyme

Smuni Turan,
my mother.

Smuni, my mother's name, is an Assyrian variant of the more common name Simone. She was born in Sare, a small village in the province of Tur Abdin in southeast Turkey. In this region, the Assyrians, a small Christian minority, have maintained their presence.

"We spoke Surayt, the language of everyone in that area. Assyrians are Syriacs, Chaldeans and Arameans; Christians in the Middle East—a very old people. When I was born, it was peaceful. About thirty or forty families, mostly related to each other, lived in our village. It was a small village without a center or streets, just some scattered houses in a barren, dry place with no rivers. Water did not come from the faucet but from wells, and we had no oven or gas. We also had no electricity, only oil lamps and a lantern to keep an eye on the animals at night. The animals lived under the house: cows, sheep, goats, chickens, turkeys, donkeys, horses, you name it. We lived basically above the stables. We children had to clean the stables out every day. The manure was saved, dried, and later spread over the land to make it fertile. My father went with my brothers to work the land with a plow drawn by an ox. Every family in the village had a vineyard and a piece of land, which they worked themselves. Some cultivated grain, others chickpeas, lentils, melons, cucumbers, pickles, tomatoes, onions, or garlic. We bought or exchanged goods with each other because we had no stores in Sare. But there were stores in Midyat, the nearest city. We went there with donkeys. No one in the village had a car, but there was a bus to the city, and I would sometimes ride in it with my father to buy salt, oil, and sugar. In turn, my father sold cows, sheep, and goats, sometimes also butter and cheese.

"I've often wondered why we had no furniture, given that there was plenty of wood in the distant forests. One of my uncles made spoons, ladles, and other utensils from that wood."

"My parents were not poor, but our life was austere. The living room was bare, without chairs, beds, or tables. Everything happened on mats on the ground. I've often wondered why we had no furniture, given that there was plenty of wood in the distant forests. One of my uncles made spoons, ladles, and other utensils from that wood. We slept in one room with our parents, on thick mattresses filled with sheep's wool. My mother refilled these, along with the pillows, every year."

Read more on page 63

Bulgur *two delicious ways: with vermicelli and with fried onion*

My parents, grandparents, and countless generations before them grew up in a region where the fertile soil was ideal for growing grain. The primary grain grown for personal consumption was wheat, which was then made into bulgur (also written as *burghul* or *bulghur*) through a method believed to have originated in ancient Mesopotamia. The wheat is boiled and dried on flat roofs in the sun; then, it is ground into various sizes, from very fine to extra coarse (pg. 32). Bulgur is known for its mild, nutty flavor, and is widely available in supermarkets today. My mother often prepares bulgur with fried vermicelli, employing a cooking technique similar to that used for rice. In addition to vermicelli, ingredients such as tomato paste, fried onion, pine nuts, and spices can complement bulgur. I find that a dollop of creamy yogurt pairs well with it, too.

SERVES 6

Bulgur with Vermicelli:

4 tablespoons (50 g) unsalted butter
½ cup (100 g) vermicelli
3 cups (600 g) medium-grain bulgur
5 ½ cups (1.3 L) water
2 teaspoons salt

Bulgur with Fried Onion:

5 ½ cups (1.3 L) water
3 cups (600 g) medium-grain bulgur
1 tablespoon tomato paste
2 ½ teaspoons salt, divided
1 tablespoon sunflower oil
1 white onion, finely chopped
1 green pepper, seeds removed, finely chopped
1 teaspoon paprika
1 teaspoon sambal (Indonesian chile paste)
½ teaspoon freshly ground pepper
½ bunch flat-leaf parsley, finely chopped

For bulgur with vermicelli: In a medium pot over medium heat, melt the butter. Fry the vermicelli, stirring, for 2 minutes or until light brown. Add the bulgur and stir continuously until each grain is coated with butter. Add the water and salt and stir well. Cover the pot, bring to a boil, and then reduce the heat to low and let the bulgur simmer for 15–20 minutes, until it has absorbed all the water. Remove the pot from the heat and let it sit 5 minutes before serving.

For bulgur with onion: In a medium pot over high heat, bring the water to a boil. Add the bulgur, tomato paste, and 2 teaspoons of the salt, and bring it back to a boil. Stir well, cover the pot, reduce the heat to low, and let the bulgur simmer for 15–20 minutes, until it has absorbed all the water. Remove from the heat and set aside.

While bulgur cooks, heat the oil in a medium skillet over medium heat. Add the onion and green pepper and sauté for 5 minutes. Add the paprika, sambal, remaining ½ teaspoon salt, and pepper, and cook for 1 minute.

Fluff the bulgur with a fork, and stir in the onion mixture and the parsley. Let the bulgur sit for 5 minutes before serving.

Qaṭiro *rich and creamy homemade yogurt*

Yogurt is a common feature on our plates. It frequently serves as a sauce or topping and often accompanies warm rice or bulgur. It can form the base of a cucumber dip (pg. 46) or a thirst-quenching drink (pg. 99). Yogurt, one of the oldest dairy products in the world, originates from ancient Mesopotamia.

For as long as I can remember, my mother has been making her own yogurt. At five in the evening, the farmer near us milks the cows. My mother then arrives with her pan to purchase the milk, fresh from the cow. That same evening, she covers a large pan of milk with a thick, heavy towel, allowing the natural bacteria to ferment. One wakes up the next morning to deliciously fresh, creamy yogurt, the flavor and texture of which are incomparable to store-bought varieties.

You can also make the yogurt with goat's milk or add flavorings like vanilla. My mother traditionally uses her fingers to gauge the milk's temperature, but I use a thermometer.

SERVES 8

½ gallon (2 l) unpasteurized (raw) whole milk (or use pasteurized whole milk but then skip the step of heating and cooling the milk)
6 tablespoons plain full-fat yogurt with active cultures

Special equipment: a large pot with a thick bottom and lid
a thick cotton cloth or towel
a cooking thermometer

If using unpasteurized raw whole milk, add the milk to the pot and turn the heat to medium-high, stirring constantly to prevent the milk from scorching. This process will take approximately 30 minutes. Warm the milk to just below a boil 185°F, checking it with the thermometer, then turn off the heat. Let the milk cool to approximately 110°F (45°C). (This is the temperature at which you can dip your finger into the milk and count to ten without getting burned.) You can speed up the cooling process by placing the pot in a sink filled with cold water for about 30 minutes.

If using pasteurized whole milk, heat the milk to 110°F (45°C).

Whisk the yogurt into the cooled milk and stir well.

Place the lid on the pot and cover the closed pot with the thick cloth. Store the pan in a draft-free area, such as an unheated oven, for at least 12 hours.

Once the yogurt is ready, you can use a paper towel to absorb the yellow layer of whey on top. Serve the yogurt immediately or keep it in the refrigerator for up to 5 days, after which it will begin to sour.

Khase da bosine *refreshing yogurt cucumber salad with dill*

Many dishes in this book range from mildly spicy to very spicy. A refreshing cucumber salad offers a welcome change. One such salad is *khase da bosine*, which literally translates to "cucumber salad." The yogurt adds a refreshing touch, while the dill enhances the flavor. Though these ingredients are common in many salads, in our version, both the yogurt and the cucumber are strained through a cloth to remove moisture. This process preserves the salad's flavor, which often intensifies after a day in the refrigerator.

SERVES 10

2 cups (500 g) Turkish or Greek yogurt (at least 10% fat)
1 garlic clove, finely chopped
½ cucumber, seeds removed, finely diced
2 tablespoons dried mint
Leaves from 2 sprigs fresh mint, finely chopped
10 sprigs dill, roughly chopped
Salt and freshly ground pepper

Special equipment: 2 pieces of cheesecloth
a medium-size strainer

Line the strainer with 1 piece of the cheesecloth, and place the strainer over a bowl to catch any drips. Pour the yogurt into the cloth-lined strainer, fold the cheesecloth ends over it, and press to remove excess liquid. Let it stand for about 30 minutes and press firmly again. Unfold the towel and transfer the yogurt to a large bowl or dish. Stir in the garlic.

While the yogurt drains, lay out the remaining piece of cheesecloth on a work surface, and add the cucumber.

Gather the ends of the cheesecloth together into a ball, and squeeze over the sink to remove liquid from the cucumber.

Add the cucumber to the yogurt along with the dried mint, fresh mint, and dill. Stir to combine, and season with salt and pepper to taste.

Rezo sh'iraye *vermicelli rice*

In my mother's pantry, you will always find a linen sack filled with at least 22 pounds (10 kg) of rice. This isn't pre-processed or quick-cooking rice. In the Assyrian community, rice, like bulgur, is a staple, and forms the base of many meals. It serves as a side dish or a filling for tomatoes or peppers; it is rolled in grape leaves or made into a pudding. As a side dish, rice is typically not eaten plain. Traditionally, it is combined with sh'iraye (vermicelli), a specialty my mother, and the women from her village, used to make themselves.

First, you fry the vermicelli with rice in butter, and only after that do you add the water. It is likely that rice was originally combined with vermicelli to enhance texture and prevent clumping. Moreover, the addition of vermicelli makes the rice soft and deliciously creamy. As children, we couldn't resist sneaking a few bites from the pan before mealtime. To be honest, I find myself still giving in to this temptation.

SERVES 4

1 tablespoon unsalted butter
Generous ½ cup (3 oz/ 90 g) vermicelli
1 ⅔ (9 oz/250 g) long-grain rice
2 cups (500 ml) water
1 teaspoon salt

In a medium pot over medium-high heat, melt the butter. Add the vermicelli and cook, stirring, for about 2 minutes, or until it turns light brown. Add the rice and continue stirring until every grain is coated with butter. Add the water and salt, and stir well. Cover the pot and bring to a boil; reduce heat to low and simmer, covered, for 15 minutes.

Check that the rice has absorbed all the water, and then remove the pot from the heat. Let the rice sit covered for 5 minutes before serving.

Gweto *white raw milk cheese*

In 1969, when my parents moved to the Netherlands, it proved to be quite the culture shock. Everything was different—the language, climate, religion, social norms, and most notably, the cuisine. In the very land renowned for its cheese, my mother could not find her favorite cheese: gweto. This white cheese is similar to Greek feta or Turkish peynir but is less fatty and not as dry. Unlike the rectangular feta or round peynir, gweto has a unique, irregular shape because each piece is hand-cut into segments.

My mother decided to make gweto herself at home. However, the traditional process requires difficult-to-obtain rennet, an enzyme mixture sourced from animal stomachs that facilitates preservation. The rennet is mixed into milk, and after a short while, the milk coagulates into curds. This method proved quite complicated without rennet, so she had to come up with an alternative.

She discovered a plant-based microbial rennet that she could add to the excellent Dutch raw milk. The curds then needed to be pressed several times using cheesecloth. This was quite a labor-intensive process, leading my mother to visit a local dairy farmer, Snuverink, in nearby Hengelo, and persuade them to produce the curd for her (they still make it for her to this day). The large Assyrian community nearby visits the farm shop daily.

Unlike some Dutch cheeses, gweto does not require any aging. After two days of brining and a brief boil, it is immediately ready for use. Raw-milk cheese often has more flavor than cheese made from pasteurized milk, and it aids digestion. In our home, this white cheese was a breakfast staple, often accompanied by cucumber, tomatoes, olives, and bread or served with jam, figs, and soft sweet rolls (pg. 196).

MAKES 9 POUNDS (4 KILOGRAMS)

2 or 3 tablespoons (40 g) salt
8 gallons (30 l) raw milk with 4.5% fat, unheated
1 teaspoon plant-based rennet

Warm the milk in a large pot and stir in the rennet. Turn off the heat and allow the mixture to sit until curds form. They should be a firm, almost rubbery texture before you proceed to the next step, which will take anywhere from 4 to 12 hours.

Next, pour the salt onto a large plate. Cut the curd into pieces of about 6 by 6 inches (15 by 15 cm) and press each one into the salt, covering all sides. Place the salted curds in a large bowl. Cover the bowl with a dish towel and then seal well with aluminum foil. Set the bowl aside for 48 hours in a dry, dark place, such as an unheated oven.

Bring a large pot of water to a boil. Remove the curds from the bowl with a heatproof slotted spoon, draining the liquid, and slip them into the boiling water, being sure not to crowd the pot. Boil for 5 minutes, and remove with a slotted spoon and transfer to a clean bowl. Repeat the process until all the cheese has been boiled. When the cheese is cool enough to handle, press each piece between your hands, squeezing out as much liquid as possible. The cheese is now ready to serve immediately.

Any leftover cheese can be stored, tightly wrapped in plastic, in the freezer for 2 to 3 months. Let it thaw, then rinse thoroughly in hot water, and then again in cold water, repeating the process a few times. Otherwise, the cheese will be too salty.

Dawqo hamiğe *pan-baked flatbread*

Bread is always on the table—at any time of the day, in more than 100 varieties and sizes. We have various ways to bake it: tanuro, from the oven; dawqo, from the pan; hamiğe, with yeast; or skawa, without yeast. It can be eaten out of hand, used to dip, or consumed along with a dish. The easiest version is dawqo, flatbread from the pan. The biggest challenge is maintaining the dough's elasticity. A little yeast helps in achieving the right texture and elasticity. Remember, the bread will be crispier if it's flatter and thinner.

MAKES 8 FLATBREADS

1 teaspoon fresh yeast or 1 ½ teaspoons active dry yeast
6 ounces (170 ml) warm water, divided
2 ½ cups (300 g) flour, plus more for dusting
½ teaspoon salt
1 tablespoon sunflower oil

In a small bowl, mix the yeast with about 5 ounces (150 ml) of the water and stir until it dissolves.

In a large bowl, combine the flour and salt. Slowly pour in the yeast mixture and mix with your hands. Knead the mixture, gradually adding the remaining water and continuing to knead until the dough is smooth, elastic, and doesn't stick to your hands. If the dough feels too dry, add more water; if too wet, incorporate more flour.

Cover the bowl with a dry dish towel and let the dough rise for 30 minutes in a warm, draft-free spot.

Dust your workspace with a little flour and divide the dough into 8 equal-sized balls. Roll each ball out into a thin circle with a rolling pin, or flatten with the palm of your hand.

Lightly brush one side of each piece of dough with the sunflower oil. Heat a medium skillet over medium heat and cook the flatbread for about 2 minutes on each side (starting with the oiled side) until golden brown. Serve the flatbreads immediately.

Yarqunto *simple Assyrian vegetable salad*

If we had a country, yarqunto would be our national salad, much like the Greek salad in Greece. This salad is simple, yet complements every dish and is a constant presence on the Assyrian menu.

SERVES 4

8 Persian cucumbers, diced
3 medium vine-ripened tomatoes, seeds removed and diced
1 red onion, thinly sliced
Juice of 1 lemon
4 tablespoons extra-virgin olive oil
2 teaspoons salt

In a large bowl, combine the cucumbers, tomatoes, and onions. Add the lemon juice, oil, and salt, and gently toss by hand until well combined. Taste and adjust the flavor with more lemon juice or salt if needed.

Dawġe *refreshing yogurt drink*

Summers in the Middle East are hot and can be particularly exhausting when working outdoors. In such conditions, there's nothing more satisfying than an ice-cold glass of dawġe (pronounced "dauree"). This is the original version of a yogurt drink, made without sugar. A hint of salt is added—a necessary luxury in such a warm climate. Popular among the Assyrians, dawġe is consumed anytime, anywhere, and is second only to black tea. It pairs delightfully with spicy food, its flavor especially enhanced by a few mint leaves. It's important to find the right balance of yogurt to water to get your preferred consistency and flavor, so adjust the ratio as you desire.

MAKES ABOUT 3 ½ cups (800 ml)

4 ½ cups (1 l) Greek yogurt
2 cups (400 ml) cold water
Leaves from 2 sprigs fresh mint, coarsely chopped
½ teaspoon salt
Ice cubes, for serving

In a large pitcher, combine the yogurt, water, mint, and salt, stirring well.

Add a few ice cubes to the pitcher and pour into glasses. Serve immediately, before the yogurt and water begin to separate.

A KLASIKOYE

The Classics

Samborakat - Tawa - Apprakhe - Fulful hashyo - Kibbeh ṣeniye - Basle hashye - Kötle - Labaniyeh - Lahmo doe tanuro - Maqloubeh - M'wothé

Smuni Turan, *my mother.*

Turan, my mother's surname, is well-known among the Assyrians. Her grandfather from her father's side, Semun Hanne Haydo Turan, was a resistance fighter during the Sayfo, the genocide during which not only Armenians, but almost all Assyrians became victims. Gawriye, her grandfather from her mother's side, and his daughter, my maternal grandmother, were the only members of their family to survive the Sayfo. His wife and all their other family members were tortured, shot, or killed in some other way.

"My mother and grandfather never wanted to discuss these experiences. They did not want us to know the extent of what they had endured; it was too painful to bring those stories to light. My mother never spoke of her murdered family members. I gathered the stories from neighbors and acquaintances. My grandfather, Semun Hanne Haydo Turan, was a hero of the resistance. During the horrors of the Sayfo, he tried to protect as many people as possible and prevent attacks on entire villages. Eventually, my grandfather was taken prisoner. He and a friend, who was Muslim, executed a daring escape from the prison by tying blankets together and jumping out of a high window. They concealed themselves in the tall wheat and corn in the fields. They were like two brothers. They trusted each other."

> "He and a friend, who was Muslim, executed a daring escape from the prison by tying blankets together and jumping out of a high window."

"They went door to door asking for bread and water, but often they had to eat grass and nettles. My mother once told me that her father pretended to be dead, lying among corpses. He endured kicks from soldiers who wanted to ensure he was truly lifeless. I could talk about this for hours, but everything about Semun is also detailed in a book written about him. There is also a Hanne Haydo award to raise awareness about the Sayfo and to preserve our culture and the Aramaic language in Tur Abdin. Even so, it is especially important for the youth to be aware of the Sayfo of 1915 and commemorate it each year. This way, the suffering of our ancestors will never be forgotten."

Read more on page 94

Samborakat *crescent moons of stuffed dough*

At an Assyrian wedding, everyone indulges in generous amounts of food and drink, and the revelry continues into the next day. The morning after the wedding, the newlyweds are called *sabahiye*, which literally means "those of the morning after." Traditionally, newlyweds are served samborakat for breakfast. These are sometimes compared to small stuffed pancakes, but they are distinctly different. Pancakes are made with batter, whereas samborakat are made with very thin dough, filled with a mixture of ground meat, onions, parsley, and spices, and then folded into the shape of a crescent moon. It really takes practice to keep the dough as thin as possible without tearing it. My mother makes at least fifty samborakat at a time and freezes the leftovers to enjoy year-round, not just on special occasions. She often craves this traditional breakfast. And who can blame her? Samborakat are irresistible. It is interesting to note that to make her samborakat, my mom still uses the first pan she bought nearly fifty years ago when she first moved out of the Middle East.

MAKES 17 SAMBORAKAT

For the filling:
2 tablespoons unsalted butter, divided
1 pound (500 g) ground beef
1 tablespoon tomato paste
1 teaspoon sambal (Indonesian chile paste)
2 teaspoons seven-spice powder
1 teaspoon paprika
2 teaspoons salt
1 teaspoon freshly ground pepper
2 white onions, finely chopped
1 bunch flat-leaf parsley, roughly chopped

For the dough:
7 ½ cups (900 g) all-purpose flour, plus an additional ¾ cup (100 g) for dusting
1 teaspoon salt
2 ½ cups (550 ml) warm water
1 tablespoon sunflower oil or melted unsalted butter, plus more for frying

Make the filling: In a large skillet over medium-high heat, melt 1 tablespoon of the butter and sauté the ground beef, breaking it up with a spoon until all moisture has evaporated. Add the tomato paste, sambal, seven-spice powder, paprika, and salt and pepper, and continue to sauté, stirring, for 1 minute. Turn off the heat, transfer the ground meat mixture to a plate, and set it aside. Do not wipe out the skillet.

In the same skillet over medium heat, melt the remaining 1 tablespoon of butter. Add the chopped onion and sauté for 5 minutes, or until the onion becomes soft and translucent. Return the sautéed ground meat mixture to the pan, stir to combine with the onion, and sauté for another 2 minutes. Turn off the heat and mix in the parsley. Let cool.

Make the dough: In a large bowl, combine the 7 ½ cups flour and salt. Add a small amount of the water to the flour and begin mixing by hand. Gradually add the rest of the water and knead the mixture into a smooth, elastic dough. Add the sunflower oil and continue to knead until the dough ball no longer sticks to your hands. If the dough is too dry, add more water; if it's too wet, add more flour.

Make and cook the samborakat: Lightly dust your work surface with the remaining ¾ cup flour, and divide the dough into 17 equal-sized balls. Roll each ball out into a thin circle, about 7 inches (18 cm) in diameter, with a rolling pin, or flatten with the palm of your hand. Spread 1 ½ tablespoons of the meat mixture over just more than half of the dough circle, leaving the bottom half and an edge of about ½ inch (1 cm) free. Fold the bottom half of the dough over the filling to create a half-moon shape. Press the edge closed with your fingers and then seal the edges with the tines of a fork. Repeat with the rest of the dough balls.

In a medium nonstick pan, melt a bit of butter over medium-high heat. Add the samborakat in one layer, and fry for about 2 minutes on each side, until golden brown. Remove with a spatula and stack them on a plate. Repeat until all samborakat are fried. Serve immediately.

Tawa *casserole with meat and vegetables*

Ask any Assyrian about their favorite dish, and there's a good chance they'll say tawa. This casserole is a quintessential Assyrian comfort food. In Aramaic, tawa means "casserole dish." When I was growing up, my mother's casserole dish was made of heavy cast iron with a thick base. She said that as a child, she saw the same dish in their clay oven. My mother still uses a cast-iron casserole dish to bake this recipe and others, always presenting it at the table with a flourish. I use a regular baking dish, although it may not have my mother's approval.

SERVES 6

2 pounds (800 g) ground beef
3 garlic cloves, finely chopped
1 white onion, finely chopped
2 green peppers, seeds removed, finely chopped
1 tablespoon tomato paste
3 teaspoons sambal (Indonesian chile paste)
2 teaspoons paprika, divided
1 tablespoon plus 1 teaspoon salt, divided
1 teaspoon freshly ground pepper
3 small eggplants, thinly sliced into rounds or half-moons
6 Roma tomatoes, thinly sliced into rounds or half-moons
1½ zucchini, thinly sliced into rounds
2½ tablespoons sunflower oil
1¼ cups (300 ml) water
1 tablespoon lemon juice
1 tablespoon extra-virgin olive oil, plus more for drizzling
1 bunch flat-leaf parsley, coarsely chopped

Special equipment: a large baking dish about 2 inches (5 cm) deep

Preheat the oven to 400°F (200°C).

In a large bowl, combine the ground beef with garlic, onion, green peppers, tomato paste, sambal, 1 teaspoon of the paprika, 1 tablespoon of the salt, and the pepper. Mix well by hand.

Begin to layer the filling in the dish in a row in this order: one slice eggplant, some ground beef mixture, one slice tomato, some ground beef mixture, one slice zucchini, some ground beef mixture, pressing firmly as you add each new ingredient. Ensure that the vegetable slices stand upright and don't exceed the height of dish's edge. Continue creating rows, alternating meat and vegetables, until the dish is filled.

Evenly drizzle the sunflower oil over the vegetables and meat. In a small bowl, combine the water, lemon juice, remaining 1 teaspoon paprika, and 1 teaspoon salt, then evenly pour over the vegetables and meat.

Lower the oven temperature to 355°F (180°C) and bake the dish for approximately 2 to 2½ hours, until the tawa is browned and the liquid is mostly absorbed. (Check at 1½ hours to ensure the tawa is not browning too fast—if it is, cover the dish with aluminum foil and continue baking.)

Drizzle the tawa with olive oil and sprinkle with chopped parsley before serving.

Apprakhe *stuffed grape leaves*

Stuffed grape leaves, filled with meat, grains, and herbs, have been a culinary tradition for thousands of years, dating back to ancient civilizations. My mother grew up among the vineyards in the Tur Abdin region, known for the best Assyrian and Aramaic wines. Even in her home in the Netherlands, she's had a grapevine in her garden, primarily to harvest fresh leaves for apprakhe (pronounced "appraagee"). The word *apprakhe* means "rolled." Apprakhe in its original form is stuffed with rice, beef or lamb, various herbs and spices like sumac and fresh mint, and drizzled with lemon juice. The stuffed grape leaves are best served warm, especially with a good glass of Tur Abdin wine, or, if that is not available, another hardy red. If you don't have access to fresh grape leaves, you can use jarred grape leaves in brine and rinse them. If you buy them in a jar, skip the soaking step.

MAKES 50 STUFFED
GRAPE LEAVES

For the leaves:
50 fresh grape leaves
1 tablespoon salt
4 ¼ cups (1 l) boiling water

For the filling:
1 cup (250 g) raw arborio rice, rinsed
½ cup (100 ml) water
½ teaspoon chili powder
1 teaspoon sumac
1 teaspoon pomegranate molasses
1 teaspoon sambal (Indonesian chile paste)
1 teaspoon lemon juice
1 tablespoon tomato paste
2 teaspoons salt
½ teaspoon freshly ground pepper
½ yellow onion, finely chopped
2 garlic cloves, finely chopped
1 green chile pepper, finely chopped
6 sprigs mint, leaves finely chopped
½ red tomato, seeded and finely chopped
½ pound (250 g) ground beef

For cooking and serving:
2 tablespoons sunflower oil
1 tablespoon salt
2 ¼ cups (525 ml) cold water
lemon wedges

Special equipment: a Dutch oven or other deep, wide pot with a lid

Make 5 stacks of 10 grape leaves each. Fold each stack in half so the tops of the leaves are enclosed. Place the 5 stacks on top of each other in a large bowl, sprinkling each with salt. Fill the bowl with the boiling water until the leaves are submerged then cover with a heavy plate. Let the leaves soak for at least 4 hours. Remove them from the water bath and allow them to drain, or gently squeeze out the water from each stack by hand. Set the leaves aside on a plate.

In a large bowl, combine all of the filling ingredients and mix well by hand.

Take a grape leaf and carefully cut off the stem. Lay the leaf flat, underside up, on a cutting board. Place a small portion of the filling in a horizontal line at the base of the leaf, leaving a small space free on either side. Roll the bottom of the leaf tightly over the filling. Fold in the left and right sides, then keep rolling toward the tip, using your palm to assist, until the leaf resembles a tightly rolled, slim cylinder. Repeat this process with the remaining grape leaves, setting the finished ones aside.

Arrange the rolled leaves closely together at the bottom of the Dutch oven. Depending on the size of your pot, there may be multiple layers. Drizzle the leaves with sunflower oil and sprinkle with the salt. Place a plate on top of the rolls to weigh them down so they will not unroll, and pour in the cold water. Cover the pot and bring to a boil over medium heat.

Reduce the heat to low and simmer for 60 minutes. At this point, the rolls should have absorbed most of the water. Remove the pan from the heat and let the rolls sit for 10 minutes before serving.

Serve warm, with lemon wedges.

Fulful hashyo *stuffed bell peppers*

I have vivid memories of my mom presenting us with a large tray of freshly baked stuffed peppers. The delicious aroma of garlic, mint, and lemon would permeate the house for hours. I always preferred the red peppers, as they were a touch sweeter, and made a beautiful contrast with the spicy filling. Regardless of your choice of bell pepper, each bite of these stuffed peppers is melt-in-your-mouth delicious.

SERVES 6

5 tablespoons sunflower oil, divided
1 ½ cups (300 g) arborio rice, rinsed
2 teaspoons salt, divided
1 ½ teaspoons freshly ground pepper, divided
1 ¼ cups (300 ml) boiling water
2 medium white onions, finely chopped
3 garlic cloves, minced
1 green chile pepper, seeded and finely chopped
1 teaspoon paprika
1 teaspoon sumac
1 tablespoon tomato paste
Juice of ½ lemon
1 tablespoon dried mint
¼ cup flat-leaf parsley, finely chopped
6 bell peppers (red, green, yellow, or orange)
1 cup cold water

In a medium pot with a lid, warm 2 tablespoons of the sunflower oil over medium-high heat. Add the rice, 1 teaspoon of the salt, and ½ teaspoon of the pepper, and stir continuously to coat each grain in oil, about 3 minutes. Add the boiling water, stir, and bring the mixture to a boil. Cover the pot, reduce the heat to low, and cook the rice until the water is absorbed, about 10 minutes. (The rice won't be tender; it will continue to cook in the oven.)

Preheat the oven to 425°F (220°C).

In a medium skillet over medium heat, warm 2 tablespoons of the sunflower oil. Add the onions, garlic, and green chile and sauté until soft, about 5 minutes. Stir in the paprika, sumac, tomato paste, and the remaining 1 teaspoon salt and 1 teaspoon pepper, then continue to sauté for another 10 minutes. Lower the heat if the mixture starts to brown too quickly.

Add the partially cooked rice to the skillet and stir to combine. Add the lemon juice, mint, and parsley. Mix well and adjust the seasoning with more salt and pepper if necessary.

Slice the tops off the bell peppers and set them aside. Remove the seeds and membranes. Pour the cold water into a baking dish that will fit all 6 peppers, and stir in the remaining 1 tablespoon sunflower oil. Stuff the peppers with the rice mixture and place them upright in the baking dish. Put the tops back on the peppers. Cover the dish with aluminum foil and place in the preheated oven.

After 30 minutes, remove the foil and check if the peppers are cooking evenly. Increase the oven temperature to 475°F (250°C) and return the dish to the oven for another 15 minutes or until the peppers completely soften. Once you take the peppers out of the oven, enjoy the aroma, and serve them warm.

Kibbeh ṣeniye *baked bulgur and ground meat pie*

Kibbeh seniye, literally translated as "ball in a round baking dish," is a prime example of a uniquely delightful way to prepare bulgur. This savory dish is composed of three layers—a layer of finely ground bulgur, a layer of ground meat mixed with pine nuts and spices, and another layer of bulgur. An attractive pattern, etched in with a knife, provides the finishing touch.

SERVES 6

For the bulgur dough:
3 cups (475 g) extra-fine-grain bulgur
2 teaspoons ground cumin
2 teaspoons ground coriander
2 teaspoons sambal (Indonesian chile paste)
1 tablespoon tomato paste
½ teaspoon salt
½ teaspoon freshly ground pepper
½ cup (100 ml) cold water

For the meat filling:
1 pound (500 g) ground beef
2 teaspoons cayenne pepper
1 teaspoon chili powder
1 teaspoon seven-spice powder
1 teaspoon paprika
1 teaspoon tomato paste
1 teaspoon salt
1 teaspoon freshly ground pepper
1 tablespoon extra-virgin olive oil
3 white onions, chopped
⅔ cup (60 g) pine nuts, toasted

⅔ cup (150 g) unsalted butter, melted, divided
Plain yogurt, for serving
A green salad, for serving

Special equipment:
a clean kitchen towel
a round metal baking dish (approximately 14.5 inches (37 cm) in diameter)

Make the bulgur dough: Place the bulgur in a large bowl and then cover it with water. Knead the bulgur with your hands, then drain the excess water. To the moist bulgur, add the cumin, coriander, sambal, tomato paste, salt, and pepper, mix to combine. Cover the bowl with the kitchen towel and set aside.

Make the meat filling: In a large skillet, brown the ground beef. Stir in the cayenne, chili powder, seven-spice powder, paprika, tomato paste, and salt and pepper. In a separate large skillet over low heat, warm the olive oil and sauté the onions until soft, about 5 minutes. Add the beef mixture to the onions and cook for an additional 10 minutes until browned and all liquid has evaporated. Stir in the toasted pine nuts, remove from heat, and let the mixture cool.

Remove the towel from the bowl of softened bulgur, add the cold water, and knead the bulgur with your hands until the moisture is absorbed. Continue kneading, adding more cold water if necessary, until a smooth dough forms. Divide the dough into two equal portions.

Preheat the oven to 400°F (200 °C).

Brush the bottom and sides of the baking dish with half the melted butter. Spread the first half of the dough evenly over the bottom of the dish. Spread the meat mixture over the dough base and gently press down.

Roll out the second half of the dough and place it over the meat mixture. To do this, it's easiest to place the dough between two sheets of parchment paper and roll it out to the size of the baking dish. Remove the top piece of parchment and gently flip the dough onto the meat mixture, then remove the second piece of parchment. Firmly press around all the edges to ensure the seams are well sealed.

Brush the top of the dough with the remaining melted butter. Cut the pie into squares with a sharp knife and bake in the oven for 60 minutes or until nicely browned.

Serve with a generous spoonful of creamy yogurt and a green salad.

Basle hashye *braised stuffed onions*

Stuffed grape leaves, peppers, zucchinis, and eggplants are universally loved and well-known. But there are other lesser known, yet equally appealing vegetables that can be stuffed and baked. Onions are a prime example. We usually fill them with a mixture of rice, vegetables, herbs, and ground meat. For a vegetarian version, you can add chickpeas or pine nuts.

SERVES 5

5 large onions (a mix of red and white)
¼ pound (80 g) ground beef
½ cup (100 g) arborio rice, rinsed
2 teaspoons red chili powder
2 teaspoons salt
2 teaspoons freshly ground pepper
2 teaspoons tomato paste
1 garlic clove, minced
2 teaspoons sumac
1 teaspoon paprika
10 sprigs flat-leaf parsley, roughly chopped
1 teaspoon dried mint

Peel the onions. Slice off 1-inch (2 cm) caps from the stem end. Slice a thin piece from the root ends so they will stand upright. Place the onions (with their caps on) root-end down in a deep pot and fill the pot with enough water so the onions are three-quarters covered. Bring to a boil over medium heat, and boil the onions for 25 minutes. Using a slotted spoon, scoop the onions out of the pot and set aside to cool, leaving the water in the pot.

In a medium skillet over medium heat, brown the ground beef, breaking it apart with a spoon until fully cooked. Add the rice, chili powder, and salt and pepper, reduce the heat to low, and cook for 5 minutes, stirring to thoroughly mix the rice with the beef.

Add the tomato paste and the remaining water from the onion pot, stir well, and increase the heat to bring the mixture to a boil. Continue cooking until all the liquid has evaporated.

Stir in the garlic, sumac, and paprika, then turn off the heat; the rice should now be half-cooked. Mix in the parsley and mint.

Using a teaspoon or a small knife, carefully hollow out the onions, leaving two outer layers intact to form a shell for stuffing. Be careful not to puncture the skin.

Stuff the onions with the ground beef mixture, pressing down firmly, and then replace the caps. Stand the onions upright in the pot containing the remaining water and add additional water (if needed) to cover the onions by three-quarters. Cover the pot and bring to a boil over high heat, then reduce the heat to low and simmer until the rice is cooked and the onions are soft, approximately 30 minutes. Season to taste with additional salt and pepper. Serve the stuffed onions warm.

Kötle *stuffed wheat pouches*

Perhaps the most beloved dish among the Assyrians is kötle (not to be confused with köfte, which is an entirely different dish). Making these seemingly simple dough pouches filled with minced meat requires significant concentration, nimble fingers, and years of practice. The trick lies in creating dough that's as thin and delicate as possible, yet flexible enough to avoid tearing. This demands a very specific kneading technique, mainly using only fingertips. Time is, therefore, the primary ingredient of this dish—you mustn't be in a rush.

Historically, kötle preparation was predominantly a female affair and an opportunity to socialize, laugh, and catch up. More importantly, it was a chance for women to learn the technique from one another. Proficiency was even considered a measure of one's household skills. While this notion might now seem outdated, being adept in kötle-making was once deemed essential for homemakers. Those times have certainly passed, but fortunately, the love for this dish has not.

MAKES 27 PIECES

For the dough:
5 cups (1.2 l) lukewarm water
3 cups (500 g) extra-fine-grain bulgur
3 cups (500 g) uncooked cracked hard wheat, fine
2 teaspoons ground coriander
1 tablespoon salt

For the filling:
1 pound (500 g) ground beef
1 tablespoon tomato paste
2 teaspoons allspice
2 teaspoons paprika
1 teaspoon chili powder
1 teaspoon cayenne pepper
4 teaspoons salt, divided
1 teaspoon freshly ground pepper
2 teaspoons unsalted butter
3 yellow onions, finely chopped
1 green chile pepper, finely chopped
1 bunch flat-leaf parsley, finely chopped

Optional (if frying):
4 tablespoons unsalted butter
2 eggs, beaten

Make the dough: In a large deep bowl, combine the water, bulgur and cracked wheat. Mix everything with your hands for about 2 minutes. With your hands, scoop out the dough bit by bit and press out the moisture. Place the pressed dough in a dry bowl. Mix in the coriander and salt, cover the bowl with a towel, and let it sit in a warm, draft-free spot for 1 hour.

Make the filling: in a medium skillet over medium heat, brown the ground beef, breaking it apart with a spoon until it is fully cooked and all the moisture has evaporated. Remove from the heat and mix in the tomato paste, allspice, paprika, chili powder, cayenne, 2 teaspoons of the salt, and the pepper. Transfer to a plate and set aside.

In the same skillet (no need to wipe it out) over medium heat, melt the butter. Add the onions and sauté for 3 minutes. Add the green chile pepper and remaining 2 teaspoons salt and cook for another 2 minutes. Add the meat mixture back into the skillet and sauté for another 3 minutes. Remove the pan from the heat, transfer the mixture to a plate to cool. Once cooled, stir in the parsley.

Assemble the pouches: Prepare a bowl of cold water to moisten your hands and then knead the wheat and bulgur mixture until it forms a sticky dough. If the dough is not coming together, carefully add a small amount of additional water and continue to knead until it forms.

Divide the dough into 27 balls about 2 inches (5 cm) in diameter. Keeping your hands moist, place a dough ball in your palm. Press down with your thumb while rotating it to create a well in the dough. The opening should be about two fingers wide. Continue to work the dough into a pouch with your index and middle finger then fill it with 1½ to 2 tablespoons of filling. Press the filling in with your fingers, being careful not to tear the dough.

With moistened fingers, use your thumb and index finger to seal the edges, forming a closed ball. Repeat this process for the remaining balls of dough.

Bring a large pot of salted water to a boil over medium heat. Carefully slip 5 to 7 stuffed dough pouches at a time into the pot. They will sink to the bottom. Make sure they don't stick to each other. Boil them until they expand and float to the surface. Remove them from the water with a slotted spoon and place them on a platter. Repeat with the remaining pouches. Serve warm.

Optional (as pictured):
Form the kötle into the shape of half-moons rather than balls and boil them as directed above. In a large skillet over medium heat, melt the butter. Brush the cooked kötle with the beaten eggs. Fry them in batches of about 7 pieces until golden brown on both sides.

Labaniyeh *yogurt with hulled wheat*

Supermarket shelves are stocked with cornflakes, muesli, oatmeal, and endless variants of breakfast cereals. Personally, I prefer our traditional labaniyeh, the original combination of yogurt and grain. In ancient Mesopotamia, people enjoyed this dish before the advent of bread baking. We eat labaniyeh for breakfast as well as at other times of the day. The hulled wheat (in our language, the word for it is *gheetee*) retains a delightful bite even when mixed with yogurt. We have both a sweet and a savory version. The sweet version is usually eaten warm in winter, while the savory one is served ice-cold, making it perfect for summer.

SERVES 6

1 quart (1 l) water
1 ¼ cups (250 g) hulled wheat (spelt or farro), rinsed and drained
2 ½ cups (600 ml) plain full-fat yogurt
2 teaspoons salt

For the sweet version:
cinnamon
granulated sugar

For the savory version:
2 garlic cloves, pressed
2 tablespoons dried mint
Ice cubes, for serving

In a medium pot over medium heat, bring the water and wheat to a boil, then reduce the heat to low and simmer, uncovered, for 45 minutes, stirring regularly. Use a spoon to skim off any foam that rises to the surface. Remove the pan from the heat.

After removing the pan from the heat, mix the yogurt and salt into the warm wheat. Divide between 6 bowls.
For the sweet version, garnish each bowl with cinnamon and sugar to taste and serve warm. For the savory version, garnish with garlic and mint and refrigerate for 30 minutes before serving. Or, if you want to serve it right away, stir 2 ice cubes into each bowl.

Lahmo doe tanuro *clay oven bread*

In the Tur Abdin region, where my mother was raised, every household baked its own bread. Instead of using modern ovens, they baked in a tanuro, a communal oven made from mud clay. The tanuro, which has had the same design for thousands of years, is shaped somewhat like a giant beehive, and houses a wood fire. It has a small hole at the bottom for airflow and a larger one at the top for access. When the fire is reduced to smoldering embers, bread dough is adhered to the oven's inner walls. The result is *lahmo doe tanuro* ("bread from the oven"), a flatbread with a light texture. People eat it with almost every meal. More precisely, it's used to scoop up and eat other foods, like stews, and to soak up sauces and clean plates. However, it is also wonderful with a little butter or cheese, which melts if the bread is hot. While our modern ovens require the dough to rise for 1 ½ hours, anyone who has tasted the crispy lahmo doe tanuro agrees it's well worth the wait. This recipe is ideal for making large batches, just like my mother does.

MAKES 12–15 LOAVES

- 2 ¼ cups (600 ml) warm water, divided
- 2 tablespoons plus 2 teaspoons fresh yeast or ¼ cup active dry yeast
- 8 cups (1 kg) flour, plus more for dusting
- 3 teaspoons nigella seeds
- 1 teaspoon salt
- 2 tablespoons sunflower oil

Pour ¾ cup (200 ml) of the warm water into a large bowl and stir in the yeast until dissolved.

Add the flour, nigella seeds, salt, and another ¾ cup (200 ml) of the water to the yeast mixture and mix by hand for about 5 minutes. Add the last ¾ cup (200 ml) water and knead for an additional 15 minutes. Next, add the sunflower oil and continue to knead until the dough is smooth and forms a soft ball. If the dough sticks to your hands, add a bit more flour.

Cover the bowl with a dry tea towel and a thick cloth (as my mother always does) and let it rise for 90 minutes in a draft-free spot until it doubles in size. Toward the end of the rising time, preheat the oven to 400°F (200°C) and line 2 baking sheets with parchment paper.

Divide the risen dough into about 12 to 15 equal-sized balls. Cover with a tea towel and set aside. Lightly dust your workspace with flour and use your palm to shape each ball into a thick round, about 5 ½ inches (14 cm) in diameter. Place the dough rounds on the lined baking sheet, leaving about 1 ¼ inches (3 cm) of space between them.

Place the baking sheets in the oven and bake for 30 minutes, or until golden brown. Repeat until all dough has been cooked. Allow the slightly crispy bread to cool a bit, and then serve—or seal well in a bag and freeze for up to 2 months.

Maqloubeh *upside-down savory pie*

While the French have their tarte tatin, an upside-down apple pie, we have maqloubeh. The name translates to "flipped over." It is a savory upside-down pie, bursting with herbs and spices. The preparation is straightforward, except for the very last part: flipping the pie onto a plate. This needs to be done in one swift move, and you only get one chance to get it right. During my childhood, this event always stirred much excitement and all seven of us kids wanted to see if the maqloubeh kept its shape. If it didn't, I would see the disappointment on my mother's face. Nonetheless, the taste was undiminished, and my mother was always determined to try again soon.

SERVES 4

- 1 ½ medium eggplants, sliced
- 3 teaspoons salt, plus more for eggplant
- 12 ounces (350 g) ground beef
- 1 yellow onion, chopped
- 2 garlic cloves, crushed
- 2 teaspoons tomato paste
- 1 teaspoon allspice
- 1 teaspoon turmeric
- 1 teaspoon ground cumin
- 1 teaspoon paprika
- 1 teaspoon chili powder
- 1 teaspoon freshly ground pepper
- 3 tablespoons sunflower oil, plus more for greasing the pan
- 4 large tomatoes, sliced
- 1 cup (200 g) arborio rice, rinsed
- 1 ¾ cups (400 ml) hot water
- ¼ cup (25 g) pine nuts, toasted

Special equipment: a Dutch oven or heavy pot approximately 9 inches (22 cm) in diameter and 3 ½ inches (9 cm) high

Lay the eggplant slices on paper towels, sprinkle them with a bit of salt, and let them rest for 15 minutes.

Meanwhile, in a large skillet over medium-high heat, brown the beef for 5 minutes, breaking it up with a spoon. Add the onion, and sauté for 3 minutes. Stir in the garlic and tomato paste, then add the allspice, cumin, turmeric, paprika, chili powder, 1 teaspoon of salt, and the pepper. Continue to cook until all liquid has evaporated.

In a separate large skillet over medium heat, warm the 3 tablespoons of sunflower oil and fry the eggplant slices for 5 minutes per side.

Grease the inside of the Dutch oven with sunflower oil. Arrange alternating slices of tomato and eggplant at the bottom of the pot, starting at the outer edge and working toward the center, allowing them to slightly overlap. Repeat with a second layer. Spread the meat mixture on top and gently press it down. Scatter the uncooked rice over the meat. Next, stir together the hot water and remaining 2 teaspoons of salt, and pour over the rice. Press the contents down with a spoon. Bring the pot to a boil over medium heat, uncovered. Cover the pot, reduce the heat to low, and cook for 25 minutes.

Check the rice, and if it is cooked, remove the pot from the heat. Remove the lid, cover with a dry tea towel, put the lid back on, and let rest for 15 minutes. Remove the lid and towel. Invert a large flat plate or serving dish onto the pot. Holding the plate and pot tightly together, swiftly and carefully flip everything over. Let the pot sit upside down for 5 minutes then lift it off the plate carefully. Sprinkle the maqloubeh with the toasted pine nuts, and serve.

M'wothé *meat and grain sausage*

Organ meats, like stomach and intestines, were described on the earliest culinary records found on clay tablets. The Mesopotamians seemed to be particularly fond of them, filling them with meat and grains. The sheep intestines in this recipe (used similarly to sausage casings) are challenging to stuff, but my mother accomplishes this task with traditional ease: by hand. This primeval version is not baked, but rather boiled in a broth of onions, allspice, lemons, and bay leaves. The recipe has a strong scent, but give it a try; you might find yourself pleasantly surprised by an ancient dish that has been enjoyed for more than four thousand years.

SERVES 5

1 ½ pounds (700 g) natural sheep intestines, thoroughly cleaned
1 cup (200 g) coarse-grain bulgur
1 cup (200 g) arborio rice, rinsed
1 pound (500 g) ground beef
1 ½ tablespoons dried mint
1 tablespoon allspice
1 tablespoon chili powder
½ tablespoon paprika
1 tablespoon salt
½ tablespoon freshly ground pepper
¼ cup (50 g) unsalted butter, melted
1 lemon, cut into wedges
1 tablespoon allspice berries
4 bay leaves
1 yellow onion, sliced

Moisten the sheep intestines with water. Divide each intestine into two and place the parts in a clean sink, leaving the ends open. Locate an opening of an intestine and gently run tap water through it, ensuring each intestine is thoroughly rinsed with cold water to remove excess saltiness. Turn the intestines inside out and rinse again. Squeeze all the air out of the intestines and lay them, inside out, in a colander. Give them one more rinse in the colander.

Fill a large bowl with water and add the bulgur and rice. Mix by hand, then drain the liquid. Add the ground beef, mint, allspice, chili powder, paprika, salt, pepper, and melted butter, and knead into the meat mixture thoroughly.

Firmly hold one end of the intestine in your fist. Use your index finger to push the intestine's opening inward, causing the outer edge to fold in. Scoop a tablespoon of stuffing into the intestine's opening and push it inward with your index finger. After filling about 4 inches (10 cm), slide this filled section toward the intestine's other end with your fingers. Repeat this process until the meat is evenly distributed along the intestine. Don't fill the intestine too much, as the stuffing will expand during cooking. Remove any air bubbles. Leave about an inch (2 cm) unfilled at both ends; tying is not necessary. Repeat with the remaining intestines.

Fill a large pot with enough water to submerge the intestines, then add the lemon, allspice, bay leaves, and onion. Bring the water to a boil, then add the intestines one at a time. Cover the pot, reduce the heat to medium, and let simmer for 50 minutes. (The aroma of this dish can be distinctive, so you may want to ensure your kitchen is well ventilated during cooking.) Take a small piece of intestine from the pot and taste it. If the rice and bulgur wheat are cooked, it is ready.

Serve this hearty dish in a bowl, accompanied by a refreshing side salad.

TIP

Push about 2 inches (5 cm) of an intestine's end inward. Insert your index finger into this end and roll the rest inward by running the tap. This will naturally turn them inside out. It is important to end with them inside out to make the stuffing process easier.

SHURBA U MUKLONÉ MBAṢHLÉ

— Soups and Stews

Tlawhé - Gerso - Hemse - Bamya - Dobo - Marga - Matfuniye faṣuliye yaroqo - Matfuniye doe farmo

Smuni Turan, *my mother.*

My mother was fortunate to enjoy a peaceful and relatively carefree childhood, especially in comparison to the tumultuous times experienced by her parents and grandparents. Her mother's kitchen, a central place in her early life, serves as the foundation for this book.

"We used to eat in a circle around a pot, all from the same dish," she fondly reminisces. "My mother would start cooking as early as four in the morning. She had to prepare food for the shepherds my parents employed, who left home at the crack of dawn. She often made lentil or chickpea soup, wheat yogurt, or white bean dishes. She baked her own bread and crafted creamy yogurt, butter, vermicelli, tomato puree, and grape molasses from our vineyard's bounty. In winter, she cooked on stoves; in summer, she lit a fire outside. My father would chop wood from the forest for this purpose. At noon, we all rested due to the heat, but we always had a warm meal consisting of fried eggs with onions, sometimes accompanied by sausages. We frequently enjoyed apprakhe, stuffed grape leaves, or tawa, a baked dish featuring eggplant, potatoes, zucchini, and tomatoes served with bulgur, rice, or bread. We drank water or a homemade yogurt drink to quench our thirst. I watched my mother closely, keenly observing her technique, especially in stuffing and folding dishes. I learned so much from her, including a trick for retrieving bread from hot ashes without burning your hands; the secret was to wrap your hands in damp cloths. Visitors often arrived unexpectedly, sometimes from other villages, but everyone was always welcome to join us for a meal—we always had plenty. Weddings were grand occasions, always held on a Sunday. My father would slaughter three or four sheep for the feast.

> "Visitors often arrived unexpectedly, sometimes from other villages, but everyone was always welcome to join us for a meal—we always had plenty."

People from the entire village and neighboring ones, including Muslims, were invited. Everyone got along harmoniously, with groups of ten men (as per tradition, the men ate first) sitting in a circle on the ground. When one finished eating, he would get up and someone else would take his place. Everyone got their turn. There weren't enough plates to serve everyone simultaneously. After eating, people would dance, sing, and celebrate. We mostly ate lamb, grains, vegetables, and legumes, all served from large pots with big spoons. Uncles, aunts, cousins—they all contributed and helped. They passed around cloths soaked in cologne for washing and drying hands. We baked lots of kleicha, sweet cookies. Together with fresh fruits, these were the only desserts. We didn't have chocolate—that only came much later in the big city."

"My favorite dishes are kötle, samborakat, and pancakes served with grape syrup. My mother even drizzled this syrup over fried eggs. It might sound strange, but it's so delicious! She had many unique dishes. Take harile, for instance—I always ask friends who are traveling to Turkey, Syria, or Lebanon to bring some back for me. Harile is a kind of nougat made from dried grape molasses. It's prepared at the beginning of September and enjoyed all winter long. Around the same time, we would make red and white wine, and of course, raki, which we would enjoy at Christmas, New Year's, and when we entertained guests for dinner. Even the women and children would join in. My uncle often drank to excess, prompting his wife to chase him with a stick. Sunday was our day of rest. Our family would don our finest clothes to go around town. On Sundays, we also brought food to the poor."

Read more on page 117

Tlawhé *traditional red lentil soup*

The Assyrians observe two major fasting periods: fifty days before Easter and ten days before Christmas. During these times, meat and dairy are forbidden. My mother would often prepare her "comfort soup," also known as tlawhé—a distinctive lentil soup flavored with fresh lemon juice. It's hearty and fragrant, truly a dish that can lift your spirits. Tlawhé is my favorite soup, and I prepare it frequently, especially in the winter. I always make too much, but the leftovers freeze well.

SERVES 6

10 ½ cups (2.5 l) water
2 cups (400 g) red lentils
¾ cup (140 g) long-grain white rice
2 tablespoons sunflower oil
1 medium white onion, finely chopped
2 large garlic cloves, minced
1 green chile pepper, seeded, finely chopped
1 medium potato, peeled and finely chopped
½ carrot, finely chopped
2 tablespoons tomato paste
1 teaspoon sambal (Indonesian chile paste) or paprika
1 teaspoon salt
1 teaspoon freshly ground pepper
Juice of ½ lemon
6 spring onions, trimmed, for serving
1 lemon, cut into 6 wedges, for serving
Bread, for serving

In a large, deep pot over medium-high heat, bring the water, lentils, and rice to a boil. Stir well, reduce the heat to low, and let the mixture simmer for 45 minutes. Skim off any foam that rises to the top.

While lentils and rice cook, in a medium skillet over medium-high heat, warm the sunflower oil and add the onion, garlic, and green pepper. Sauté until soft and translucent, about 5–10 minutes, reducing the heat if the vegetables are browning too quickly.

Add the sautéed onion mixture and the potato, carrot, tomato paste, and sambal to the pot with the lentils and rice. Stir in the salt, pepper, and lemon juice. Continue simmering until the lentils, rice, and vegetables are tender. Check the consistency of the soup; it should not be too thick. If necessary, add extra boiling water with some additional salt and pepper to taste.

Divide the soup between 6 bowls, and serve with the spring onions and lemon wedges. The onion is eaten raw, and the lemon juice lifts the soup to a whole new level. And don't forget the bread for dipping!

Gerso *warm and creamy wheat*

Gerso is a dish made from coarse cracked wheat and has been prepared since agriculture began. However, gerso is also a modern dish, as it is vegan and whole-grain. It is crucial that you choose the right grain in the supermarket. I usually buy wheat groats from Syrian or Turkish stores, but even then, I always have to carefully check the packaging to make sure I have the right one. Gerso is a traditional dish that my father would often prepare if my mother was away. Despite its simplicity, it's a delicious dish, and the ingredients are always available.

SERVES 8

- 4 tablespoons plus 1 teaspoon extra-virgin olive oil (54 ml), divided
- 1 white onion, finely chopped
- 2 green chile peppers, finely chopped
- 1 red chile pepper, seeded, finely chopped
- ½ teaspoon paprika
- ½ teaspoon four-season pepper (a blend of black, white, green, and pink peppercorns), or ½ teaspoon freshly ground black pepper
- 1 teaspoon ground coriander
- 1 tablespoon plus ½ teaspoon salt, divided
- 1 tablespoon tomato paste
- 10 ½ cups (2.5 l) water
- 3 cups (500 g) coarse wheat groats or cracked wheat
- 1 bunch flat-leaf parsley, finely chopped, for garnish

In a medium skillet over low heat, warm 4 tablespoons of the olive oil. Add the onion and green and red peppers and sauté, stirring regularly, until soft and translucent, about 10–12 minutes. Add the paprika, four-season pepper, coriander, and ½ teaspoon of the salt, and sauté for 1 more minute. Turn off the heat, add the tomato paste, and stir into the onion-pepper mixture.

In a large pot, bring the water to a boil. Add the remaining 1 tablespoon of salt and stir until dissolved. Add the wheat groats, stirring well. Cook for 15 minutes, skimming off any foam that rises to the top. Reduce the heat to low, stir in the remaining 1 teaspoon olive oil, and let the groats simmer until tender, about 20 minutes. Continue stirring until the mixture is soft but not too thick.

Stir the onion-pepper mixture into the cooked wheat. Serve warm, garnishing each serving with parsley.

Hemse *chickpea soup*

Chickpeas, along with lentils, are among the legumes that have been eaten since the earliest times. Clay tablets excavated in Mesopotamia mention them, and they continue to be increasingly used in a variety of dishes today. The Assyrians, for instance, create a savory, spicy, and fragrant soup from chickpeas. The preparation does require some patience, as the chickpeas need to be soaked and then boiled. But the result is doubly rewarding.

SERVES 8

- 3 ½ cups (700 g) dried chickpeas
- 4 tablespoons sunflower oil, divided
- 1 medium white onion, finely chopped
- 1 garlic clove, finely chopped
- 1 green chile pepper, seeded, finely chopped
- 1 red bell pepper, finely chopped
- 2 teaspoons freshly ground pepper
- 4 ¼ cups (1 l) plus 3 ½ cups (800 ml) water, divided
- 2 tablespoons tomato paste
- 1 teaspoon sambal (Indonesian chile paste)
- 1 teaspoon paprika
- 1 tablespoon lemon juice
- 1 tablespoon salt
- 1 bunch flat-leaf parsley or cilantro, roughly chopped, for garnish
- Lemon wedges, for serving
- Flatbread, for serving

Place the dried chickpeas in a large deep pot and add cold water to cover the chickpeas by several inches. Let them soak for 2 hours and then drain. Dry out the pot.

In the same pot over low heat, warm 2 tablespoons of the sunflower oil and fry the chickpeas for 10 minutes over low heat, stirring well to prevent them from sticking to the bottom or burning.

In a large skillet over low heat, warm the remaining 2 tablespoons of sunflower oil, add the onion, and sauté until soft and translucent, about 5 minutes. Add the garlic, green chile pepper, red bell pepper, and ground pepper, and cook for several more minutes, until vegetables have softened. Remove from heat and scrape the onion mixture into the pot with the chickpeas. Turn the heat to low, and add 4 ¼ cups of the water. Add the tomato paste, sambal, paprika powder, lemon juice, and salt. Stir well, and increase the heat to bring everything to a boil. Reduce the heat to low, cover the pot, and simmer on low heat for 1 ½ hours.

Add the remaining 3 ½ cups of water to maintain the consistency of the soup. Begin tasting every 20 minutes to check if the chickpeas are cooked. If necessary, add more water, and continue to check the doneness. This can take up to 2 more hours. Taste and adjust seasonings as necessary.

When the soup is ready, serve it in deep bowls, sprinkled with parsley or coriander, and accompanied by a lemon wedge and flatbread.

Bamya *okra stew with beef*

I absolutely adore okra; they are crunchy, flavorful vegetables that resemble small peppers or mini zucchini. If you can't get fresh, frozen okra also works well for this recipe because it is available year-round and has a long shelf life. Make sure they are small and firm, as this indicates they are tender and delicious. The Assyrian word for okra is *bamya*, which is also the name of this fragrant stew.

SERVES 6

1 tablespoon unsalted butter
1 pound (500 g) beef stew meat, cubed
5 garlic cloves, finely chopped
½ teaspoon paprika
½ teaspoon ground coriander
2 teaspoons salt
½ teaspoon freshly ground pepper
4 ¼ cups (1 l) boiling water
2 bay leaves
1 tablespoon extra-virgin olive oil
1 white onion, finely chopped
8 Roma tomatoes, finely chopped
1 ½ tablespoons tomato paste
½ teaspoon chili flakes
1 pound (400 g) small okra, fresh or frozen, coarsly chopped
Cooked rice or bulgur, for serving

In a Dutch oven or large pot over high heat, melt the butter and sear the beef on all sides. Add the garlic, paprika powder, coriander powder, and salt and pepper, and cook for 1 more minute. Add the boiling water and bay leaves, and reduce heat to low. Simmer for 2 ½ hours, or until the meat is tender. If the liquid evaporates too quickly, add additional water.

While beef cooks, in a large skillet over medium-high heat, warm the oil, add the onion, and sauté until soft, about 5 minutes. Add the tomatoes and sauté for another 25 minutes over low heat. Mix in the tomato paste and chili flakes.

Add the onion mixture to the meat and continue to simmer over low heat for 15 minutes.

If using frozen okra, place it in a colander and run it under cold water until defrosted. Add the okra to the stew simmer for another 15 minutes.

Serve the okra stew warm with rice or bulgur on the side.

Dobo *lamb leg with garlic and spice*

Legend has it that Assyrian kings in their palaces greatly enjoyed dobo, a sumptuous stuffed leg of lamb. Precious spices fill the holes punctured into the leg, making it a royal feast. I recall my mother preparing dobo when important guests, usually a cherished uncle or aunt, came to visit. Thus, it was always a small celebration that required some patience, because dobo needs several hours to simmer on the stove. In ancient times, the cooking took the whole day, but these days, two hours of cooking usually suffices if you prep the meat the night before and keep it in the fridge overnight. Even kings must keep up with the times!

SERVES 5

15 garlic cloves, sliced
1 tablespoon paprika
1 tablespoon allspice
1 ½ tablespoons salt
1 tablespoon freshly ground pepper
1 bone-in lamb leg, about 3 ½ pounds (1.5–1.7 kg), cleaned and trimmed of fat
2 tablespoons tomato paste
1 ½ tablespoons unsalted butter
1 ¼ cups (300 ml) warm water
½ tablespoon whole cloves
1 tablespoon allspice berries
4 bay leaves
Cooked bulgur, for serving

In a small bowl, stir together the garlic, paprika, allspice, and salt and pepper.

With a small, sharp knife, make several ½-inch deep cuts in the lamb leg. Push the seasoned garlic slices into the cuts. Rub the remaining spice mixture and the tomato paste onto the leg, then wrap it in plastic wrap. Store it in the refrigerator for at least 6 hours to allow the flavors to infuse the meat. Remove the leg from the refrigerator 1 hour before cooking to bring it to room temperature.

Remove the plastic wrap from the lamb. In a wide, deep Dutch oven or other heavy pot over high heat, melt the butter and sear the lamb on all sides. Pour the warm water into the pan and add the cloves, allspice berries, and bay leaves. Reduce the heat to medium and simmer for 15 minutes. Reduce the heat to medium-low, cover the pot, and continue to simmer for an additional 90 minutes or more, turning the leg occasionally and adding more water if necessary, until the meat is cooked.

Dilute the juices at the bottom of the pan with a small glass of hot water to create a sauce, and serve over bulgur.

Marga *spicy onion beef stew*

When I was young, I anticipated marga for weeks in advance. Marga may sound like a girl's name, but for the Assyrians, it's a spicy stew with beef and onion. My mother would only make it for Christmas or after the fasting period. Today, the special anticipation has somewhat diminished because I make marga throughout the year—it's too good to only have on special occasions. This recipe uses beef, but it's just as delicious with lamb, mutton, or even goat.

SERVES 8

For the beef:
1 tablespoon unsalted butter
1 pound (500 g) beef stew meat, cubed
1 teaspoon salt
2 teaspoons freshly ground pepper
1 teaspoon chili powder
2 bay leaves

For the onion mixture:
2 tablespoons extra-virgin olive oil
8 large white onions, coarsely chopped
4 teaspoons salt
1 teaspoon freshly ground pepper
1 teaspoon paprika
1 teaspoon chili powder
1 green chile pepper, seeded and finely chopped
1 red bell pepper, finely chopped
2 vine tomatoes, seeded and finely chopped
1 (6-ounce) can tomato paste
Juice of ½ lemon
3 cups (700 ml) water

Bread, bulgur, or rice, for serving

Cook the beef: In a Dutch oven or other large heavy pot over medium-high heat, melt the butter and brown the meat on all sides. Season the meat with the salt, pepper, and chili powder. Stir in the bay leaves, reduce the heat to low, and let the meat simmer gently on low heat in its own juices for about 90 minutes. Check occasionally to ensure there's enough liquid in the pan and add a small amount of water if necessary.

Make the onion mixture: While the beef cooks, in a large pot over medium heat, warm the olive oil and sauté the onions until translucent, about 5 minutes, stirring occasionally. Add the salt, pepper, paprika, and chili powder and continue to sauté for 1 more minute. Add the green pepper, red bell pepper, tomatoes, tomato paste, lemon juice, and water, then increase the heat to bring the mixture to a boil. Reduce the heat to low and simmer for 20 minutes, stirring occasionally.

Using a slotted spoon, remove the stewed meat from the pot and add to the onion mixture. Stir well, and simmer gently for another 50 minutes on very low heat to meld the flavors.

Serve with bread, bulgur, or rice.

Matfuniye faṣuliye yaroqo
green bean and lamb stew

Matfuniye faṣuliye yaroqo, a delicious lamb and green bean stew, could awaken any Assyrian. It's a signature dish and naturally, my mother makes the best version. I prefer it served with vermicelli, but it's also perfect comfort food when paired with fresh bread.

SERVES 6

For the lamb:
2 tablespoons unsalted butter, divided
1 pound (500 g) lamb stew meat, tendons removed, cut into strips
1 tablespoon salt
1 tablespoon freshly ground pepper
3 cups (525 ml) water

For the vegetables:
2 ½ pounds (1 kg) green beans
3 tablespoons sunflower oil
1 large white onion, finely chopped
2 garlic cloves, finely chopped
3 Roma tomatoes, diced
3 ½ ounces (100 g) tomato paste
3 teaspoons lemon juice
2 teaspoons paprika
1 red chile pepper, seeded, finely chopped
1 tablespoon salt
2 tablespoons freshly ground pepper
3 cups (525 ml) water
1 tablespoon sambal (Indonesian chile paste)

Rezo sh'iraye (vermicelli rice, pg. 49) or bread, for serving

Cook the lamb: In a Dutch oven or other large heavy pot over medium heat, melt 1 tablespoon of the butter, add the lamb, and brown it on all sides. Pour off any juices from the pot. Sprinkle the meat with the salt and pepper and add the remaining 1 tablespoon of butter to the pot, along with the water (it should barely cover the meat—add more if necessary). Bring to a boil, then reduce the heat and simmer for 1 to 1 ½ hours, with the lid slightly ajar, until the meat is tender. Skim off any foam that floats to the top. Remove the meat to a plate and cover with aluminum foil to keep it warm. Pour any liquid out of the pot, but don't wash the pot.

Prep and cook the vegetables: While the lamb cooks, wash the beans and remove the stem ends. Soak them in a bowl of cold water with some salt for 30 minutes.

In the previously-used pot, warm the sunflower oil over medium heat and sauté the onion until translucent, approximately 5 minutes. Remove the green beans from the water and add them to the pot. Sauté for 2 minutes. Add the garlic and cook for 5 minutes or until the beans are bright green. Add the tomatoes, tomato paste, lemon juice, paprika, red pepper, salt, pepper, and water, stirring well. Add the lamb and the sambal and stir again. Cover the pot, reduce the heat to low, and simmer for about 40 minutes, until the beans are just tender.

Serve warm with vermicelli rice or bread.

Matfuniye doe farmo — *oven-baked zucchini stew*

Sometimes, I don't have time to get to the grocery store. In such cases, I optimistically peer into the fridge, hoping to find something edible. Fortunately, in the vegetable drawer, there are often onions, peppers, and zucchini, all of which can be turned into something delicious—this recipe, for example. *Matfuniye doe farmo* translates to "vegetable stew from the oven"—it's a dish that can incorporate almost any ingredient you have on hand. The base is a sauce of tomato paste, lemon, and garlic. After that, you can let your imagination run wild—vegetables, meat—all are allowed. Personally, I find this vegetarian variant with zucchini very tasty, and, of course, it's simpler and quicker to prepare without meat.

I also love making this dish with friends. Everyone chops something; then we let the stew simmer while enjoying a glass of wine together. It's an easy dish but be sure to take the time to properly sauté the zucchini. You can hardly go wrong; matfuniye doe farmo is always delightful. And, like any stew, it's even better the next day.

SERVES 5

- 6 mini zucchini, sliced into ½-inch (1 ½-cm) rounds
- 1 tablespoon salt, plus more for zucchini
- 2 tablespoons sunflower oil, plus more for the baking dish
- 1 large yellow onion, sliced into rings
- 4 garlic cloves, finely chopped, divided
- 1 red pepper, seeded and sliced
- 1 green chile pepper, sliced into rings
- 4 vine tomatoes, sliced
- 2 tablespoons tomato paste
- 1 ¼ cup (275 ml) warm water
- Juice of ½ lemon
- 2 teaspoons sambal (Indonesian chile paste)
- 2 teaspoons freshly ground pepper

Special equipment: a baking dish approximately 8 x 10 x 3 inches (20 x 25 x 8 cm) in diameter

Place the zucchini slices on paper towels; sprinkle them with salt and let them sit for 10 minutes.

Preheat the oven to 425°F (225°C).

In a medium nonstick pan over medium heat, warm the sunflower oil and sauté the zucchini slices for about 6 minutes, until golden brown on both sides. Remove them from the pan and set aside. In the same pan, sauté the onions until translucent, about 2 minutes.

Grease the baking dish with sunflower oil and cover the bottom with a layer of zucchini. Sprinkle a third of the finely chopped garlic over it. Make a second and then a third vegetable layer from the pepper, chile pepper, tomato, onion, and zucchini, sprinkling each layer with a third of the finely chopped garlic.

In a small bowl, combine the tomato paste, warm water, lemon juice, sambal, 1 tablespoon salt, and pepper, then pour the mixture over the vegetables.

Cover the dish with aluminum foil and bake in the preheated oven for 20 minutes. Remove the foil and bake for another 15 minutes.

Served with a plate of vermicelli rice (pg. 49), bulgur, or freshly baked bread.

YARQUNWOTHO, YARIQUTHO U SHARKO

—— Vegetables and More

Qar'ukkat - Ballo' - Faṣuliye ḥeworo - Itj - Hemse thine - Mujadarah - Makdous - Muhammara - Be'é semoqe - Yarqunto da saldemee - Yarqunto di lhana - Yarqunto fattoush - Yarqunto semaqto - Yarqunto tabouleh

Smuni Turan, *my mother.*

A marriage proposal abruptly interrupted my mother's youth. She was only sixteen when she wed, which was not unusual in that era and culture. And, despite her young age, the marriage turned out to be a tremendous success.

"One day, a cousin of my father visited us. He had an attractive son with blue-green eyes and he thought I was a suitable bride for him. Habib, as my father was called, was instantly intrigued. I was only sixteen, practically still a child, and it caught me by surprise. I was not ready. I did not want a husband and exclaimed in disbelief, 'Have you all lost your minds?' Still, I eventually agreed. Our families both had very good reputations, and I didn't want to ruin them both by turning him down. Thus, I married Garibo in 1966. He arrived on a white horse, with guns firing in the air to celebrate. I was wearing a beautiful light blue and pink dress, adorned with gold thread. My husband had the fabric specially brought from Syria. Everyone said I was the most beautiful bride. Guitar music played and we danced in circles on the flat rooftops of the houses. The celebration lasted for three days."

> ## "Guitar music played and we danced in circles on the flat rooftops of the houses. The celebration lasted for three days."

"We moved to my husband's village, Kaferbe, about a three-hour walk away—we always walked everywhere. We settled into a beautiful house with magnificent rooms. My husband had been a cook during his time in the military. He prepared meals for entire regiments in large pots. Even throughout our marriage, he often cooked. He would also help with the dishes, hanging the laundry, vacuuming, and performing other household chores. This was quite unusual in our culture, but he did it nonetheless. Assyrian customs can be quite old-fashioned, but I chose not to conform and he always included me in everything. For instance, in a symbol of traditional gender roles, many women in our church still walk behind their husbands. I never did that; I always walked beside my husband."

"Sadly, he passed away in 2004 in a car accident. I still ache for him every day because he was a truly charming, kind, and dependable man. My marriage was a great success."

Read more on page 152

Qar'ukkat *scrambled eggs with zucchini and garlic*

Qar'ukkat simply means "zucchini." In fact, this dish could also be called *tumo*, which translates to "garlic," as it's another crucial ingredient (so consider yourself forewarned). I've heard that in warmer climates, the infamous garlic breath is less noticeable. In our country, it's advisable to consume parsley or mint to neutralize the scent. Nonetheless, don't let this discourage you from enjoying qar'ukkat abundantly and frequently, at any time of the day. Because it contains egg, many people enjoy qar'ukkat for breakfast, but it's also a great appetizer or side dish. If you prefer, you can omit the eggs and serve it as a dip.

SERVES 4

2 tablespoons extra-virgin olive oil
2 zucchini, trimmed and diced
2 garlic cloves, minced
2 green bell peppers, finely chopped
1 teaspoon Aleppo pepper
Salt and freshly ground pepper
3 eggs
½ bunch flat-leaf parsley, coarsely chopped

In a large skillet over low heat, warm the oil and sauté the zucchini on low heat until golden brown and soft, approximately 25 minutes.

Add the garlic and green peppers, and sauté for 2 minutes, until they are soft but not browned. Stir in the Aleppo pepper and season with salt and pepper to taste.

In a medium bowl, briefly whisk the eggs with a fork. Add the eggs to the pan and stir gently for 3 minutes until they are firm.

Divide the dish among 4 plates, and garnish with the parsley.

Yarqunto semaqto *roasted red cabbage with feta, mint, and pistachios*

Red cabbage is popular in modern vegetarian restaurants, but my mother has been preparing it since my childhood. She made *yarqunto semaqto*, "red salad," by roasting and caramelizing red cabbage in the oven. This was topped with white cheese, green onions, pistachios, mint, and pomegranate molasses. The beauty of this dish is that each bite brings a hint of mint, a sweet and sour tang from pomegranate molasses, a kick from the Aleppo pepper, the sharp taste of green onions, and the sweetness of the caramelized cabbage. It's a delight not only in flavor but also in appearance.

SERVES 5

4 tablespoons extra-virgin olive oil
1 tablespoon lemon juice
1 teaspoon paprika
1 teaspoon Aleppo pepper
1 teaspoon salt
1 teaspoon freshly ground pepper
1 red cabbage, sliced into 5 rounds of about 1.2 inches (2 cm)
5 tablespoons Greek yogurt
5 tablespoons pomegranate molasses
2 ½ ounces (70 g) feta or other firm white cheese, cubed
¼ cup (20 g) pistachios, toasted
Leaves from 5 sprigs mint, coarsely chopped
2 green onions, white parts only, sliced thinly

Preheat the oven to 400°F (210°C) and line a baking sheet with parchment paper.

In a small bowl, whisk together the olive oil, lemon juice, paprika, Aleppo pepper, and salt and pepper.

Arrange the cabbage slices on the prepared baking sheet and brush the top side of each with the marinade. Roast for 30 minutes.

Spoon the yogurt evenly onto 5 plates. Place a warm slice of cabbage atop the yogurt. Drizzle with the pomegranate molasses.

Garnish the plates with the feta, pistachios, mint, and green onions. Serve immediately.

Yarqunto tabouleh *tabouleh parsley salad*

I truly love this dish. The key is to finely chop the ingredients and balance the olive oil and lemon juice correctly. Once you achieve this, you get a refreshing and subtly tangy parsley salad with a refined flavor. Variations abound. In Lebanon, more parsley is favored, while in Syria, they prefer more bulgur. In my mother's region, the colors of the salad matter most.

SERVES 6

1 cup (150 g) fine-grain bulgur
¾ cup (190 ml) cold water
1 tablespoon spicy paprika paste
2 Roma tomatoes, finely chopped
1 head baby romaine lettuce, finely chopped
5 green onions, white part only, thinly sliced
½ cup (20 g) mint, leaves finely chopped
1 cup (45 g) flat-leaf parsley, finely chopped
¼ cup (10 g) extra-virgin olive oil
Juice of 2 lemons
2 teaspoons salt
1 teaspoon freshly ground pepper

In a large bowl, stir together the bulgur and water. Let it sit for approximately 10 minutes, or until all the water is absorbed.

Stir the paprika paste into the bulgur. Add the tomatoes, lettuce, green onions, and mint. Mix well and set aside.

Just before serving, add the parsley, olive oil, and lemon juice. Mix well and season with the salt and pepper. Taste and adjust seasonings, including more lemon juice if desired.

Itj *bulgur balls*

These bulgur balls are our version of a delicious savory appetizer. Made of wheat and vegetables, they're ideal for vegetarians and vegans. This dish is essentially a bulgur salad kneaded into a firm dough with spicy herbs and sprinkled with lemon juice and then shaped into balls or cigar shapes. You can also simply spread the mixture flat on your plate. I prefer to enjoy itj (pronounced "eetch") with drinks, but my family often savors it as a snack.

MAKES 20 BALLS

- 2 tablespoons extra-virgin olive oil, divided
- 1 red onion, finely chopped, divided
- 1 ½ cups (9 ounces or 250 g) fine-grain bulgur
- 4 tablespoons (2 ounces or 60 g) tomato paste
- 1 ½ teaspoons ground cumin
- 1 teaspoon paprika
- 2 teaspoons sambal (Indonesian chile paste)
- 1 teaspoon salt
- 1 teaspoon freshly ground pepper
- 2 cups (450 ml) boiling water
- ½ red bell pepper, seeded and finely chopped
- 6 sprigs curly parsley, finely chopped, plus more for garnish
- Juice of 1 lemon

In a deep pot, warm 1 tablespoon of the olive oil over medium heat. Add half the onions and sauté until softened, about 5 minutes. Set the rest of the onions aside.

Reduce the heat to low, then stir in the bulgur, tomato paste, cumin, paprika, sambal, and salt and pepper. Pour in the boiling water, stir well, and increase the heat to bring to a boil. Turn off the heat and let the bulgur cool for 15 minutes.

Empty the cooled bulgur into a large bowl and add the red bell pepper, remaining 1 tablespoon olive oil, parsley, and the chopped raw onions. Stir well and season with salt and pepper to taste. Knead the itj mixture with your hands until it forms a smooth and even dough. Shape it into balls, or cylinders about 3 inches long.

Transfer the itj to a platter and drizzle with the lemon juice. Sprinkle with extra parsley, if desired.

Hemse thine   *creamy hummus with tahini*

Hemse, or "chickpeas" in our Aramaic language, was a staple in ancient Mesopotamia, and likely even before that. In Arabic, a language with many borrowings from Aramaic, this legume is called *hummus*, which has also become the name for the paste or puree made from it throughout the Middle East. In the West, hummus has become exceptionally popular. The available variations are endless, with flavors like roasted pepper, garlic, pumpkin, and more. Personally, my favorite is still the basic recipe. Because I don't always have time to soak and cook dried chickpeas, I often use canned chickpeas, as in this recipe, and it works just as well.

SERVES 4

1 ½ cups (310 g) canned chickpeas with their liquid
Juice of ½ lemon
1 garlic clove, peeled
4 ice cubes
1 tablespoon tahini
1 teaspoon salt
chili powder, sweet paprika, roasted pine nuts, sesame seeds, chopped parsley, or whole chickpeas, for garnish (optional)
Flatbread, for serving

In a blender or food processor, combine the chickpeas with their liquid, lemon juice, garlic clove, ice cubes, tahini, and salt, and purée for 3 to 5 minutes, until the hummus attains a smooth and creamy texture. Taste and adjust the seasoning with additional salt or lemon juice. Add an additional ice cube if a thinner consistency is desired.

Serve the hummus in a bowl, sprinkled with any of the optional garnishes, and accompanied by warm, inviting flatbread.

Mujadarah *lentils and rice with caramelized onions*

I find myself increasingly cooking dinner for friends who prefer to eat vegan food, and I often choose mujadarah (pronounced "me-zha-dah-rah") for this purpose. It is not only delicious but also very simple (and inexpensive!) to make. You really only need three ingredients: lentils, rice, and a large amount of onions. Six are mentioned in the recipe, but feel free to use eight, or even ten: the more onions, the better. The trick is to caramelize some of the onions and cook the rest until they are crispy, just shy of being burned. I like to add some pomegranate seeds with a dollop of plant-based yogurt or hummus to finish the dish.

SERVES 4

4 ½ cups (1 l) water, divided
1 cup (7 oz or 175 g) dried green lentils, rinsed
½ tablespoon unsalted butter
1 cup (6 ½ oz or 175 g) basmati rice
1 tablespoon ground cumin
½ tablespoon salt
½ tablespoon freshly ground pepper
3 tablespoons sunflower oil
6 white onions, thinly sliced
5 tablespoons Greek yogurt (or a plant-based alternative), for garnish
5 tablespoons pomegranate seeds, for garnish

In a Dutch oven, bring 2 ½ cups (600 ml) of the water to a boil. Add the lentils, reduce the heat to low, and simmer for 15 minutes. Drain the lentils and set aside.

In the same pot over medium heat, melt the butter. Add the rice, cumin, salt, and pepper, and stir until all the grains are coated with the butter. Add the remaining 2 cups (400 ml) water and bring to a simmer. Add the cooked lentils, reduce the heat to low, cover the pot, and cook for 15 minutes. Remove from heat and let the rice and lentils rest for 5 minutes.

While the rice and lentils cook, in a large deep skillet over high heat, warm the oil for 3 minutes. Add the sliced onions and reduce the heat to medium-low, stirring every few minutes until the onions caramelize and turn brown. This should take about 15 to 20 minutes.

After the rice and lentils rest, stir in half of the caramelized onions. Serve the mujadarah warm, topped with the remaining onions and garnished with yogurt and pomegranate seeds.

Makdous *stuffed baby eggplants*

The most significant aspect of my mother's rural lifestyle was living in harmony with the seasons. Autumn meant preparing for winter: meat was salted and fruits and vegetables were dried and canned. Of all these preparations, makdous may be the finest example. It takes some time, but the reward is a treat to enjoy throughout winter or even the entire year. It all begins with baby eggplants, which have fewer (bitter) seeds than the larger varieties. The secret to excellent makdous is extracting all the moisture from the eggplant. The eggplants, together with other ingredients, are preserved by being submerged in spiced olive oil rich with garlic. It's the perfect dish when unexpected guests drop in—if you have managed to resist devouring it all beforehand!

MAKES 10 STUFFED BABY EGGPLANTS

10 baby eggplants
Salt
1 ½ cups (140 g) roughly chopped walnuts
5 garlic cloves, finely chopped
2 red bell peppers, seeded, finely chopped
1 tablespoon sambal (Indonesian chile paste)
Extra-virgin olive oil

Special equipment: a clean glass jar with lid with a capacity of about 50 fluid ounces (approximately 6 ½ cups or 1500 ml)

Remove the eggplant stems, but leave the crowns. Wash the eggplants and place them in a deep pot. Place a heavy heatproof plate on top of the eggplants to keep them submerged, then fill the pot with water until they're completely covered.

Turn the heat to medium and cook the eggplants for about 10 to 15 minutes, until they are tender but still retain some firmness. Remove the eggplants from the pan with a slotted spoon and run them under cold water to cool them down. Remove the crowns.

Make a small lengthwise cut in the center of each eggplant, without cutting completely through. Generously salt the inside and outside of the eggplants. Place them cut-side down in a deep dish or bowl and cover them with a kitchen towel. Place a heavy pan or cutting board on top of the towel, ensuring all the eggplants are pressed firmly to help extract the moisture. Let the eggplants stand for at least one day at room temperature, draining any excess liquid regularly.

To prepare the filling, in a medium bowl, stir together the walnuts, garlic, red pepper, chili paste, and 1 teaspoon olive oil. Once all moisture has been extracted from the eggplants, fill each one with a teaspoon of filling and place them, filled side up, against each other in a large sterilized, dry jar. Fill the jar with olive oil until the eggplants are well submerged. Seal the jar and place it in the refrigerator, allowing the eggplants to marinate and absorb the flavors. Eat within 7 days.

Yarqunto da saldemee *beet salad with chickpeas*

This salad encapsulates why our cuisine is so beloved. The name *yarqunto da saldemee* ("salad of red beets") belies the rich diversity within the dish, as it encompasses a variety of flavors and ingredients beyond beets. It offers a blend of tastes, scents, and colors, presenting a palette that ranges from sour to sweet and from spicy to savory. The ingredients listed below used to grow in my mother's rural garden, and they remind her of her childhood every time she prepares this dish. As a child, she found the combination of all these flavors and colors to be utterly enchanting. For that reason alone, yarqunto da saldemee often graces her table.

SERVES 5

1 tablespoon plus 5 teaspoons extra-virgin olive oil, divided
¾ cup (130 g) canned chickpeas, drained and rinsed
2 garlic cloves, finely chopped
Juice of 1 lime
2 teaspoons cinnamon
⅔ cup (60 g) roughly chopped walnuts
4 medium beets (500 g), cooked and thinly sliced
4 figs, quartered (or grapes, or pear slices)
Salt and freshly ground pepper
10 sprigs cilantro, roughly chopped

In a medium skillet over medium heat, warm 1 tablespoon of the olive oil and sauté the drained chickpeas for 10 minutes, stirring occasionally.

In a small bowl, whisk together the remaining 5 teaspoons olive oil and the garlic, lime juice, and cinnamon. Add this mixture and the walnuts to the chickpeas and sauté for 1 additional minute. Stir well and turn off the heat.

Arrange the beets and figs on a large, flat dish, and scatter the warm, spiced chickpeas on top. Sprinkle the salad with salt and pepper to taste and the chopped cilantro.

Be'é semoqe *natural red eggs*

Every year, months before Easter, my mother would invariably remind us to save our onion skins instead of discarding them. She would use them to naturally dye eggs red on Good Friday, two days before Easter. In Assyrian culture, red-dyed eggs are deeply symbolic. The egg yolk represents new life, light, and the sun. The egg white symbolizes peace and purity, and the red color signifies the blood of Jesus, shed when he was crucified to deliver mankind. As a child, I sometimes envied other children their eggs of many colors, while we only had red ones. Now, I find this natural way of dyeing to be beautiful and special.

MAKES 12 EGGS

9 cups (2 l) water
dry outer skins from 9 red onions
1 tablespoon salt
12 white eggs

In a deep pot, combine the water, onion skins, and salt, and bring to a boil over high heat. Reduce the heat to low and simmer for 10 minutes.

Turn off the heat. Using a spoon, gently lower the eggs one by one into the pot, ensuring they rest on the bottom, and then layer the onion skins over them. Bring the mixture to a boil again, reduce heat to medium, and simmer the eggs for 10 minutes.

Turn off the heat and let the eggs sit in the pot for 25 minutes. Remove with a spoon and place them on a paper towel to dry.

Muhammara *spicy roasted pepper dip with pomegranate*

I would never tell my mother, but the most delicious muhammara I ever tasted was during a trip through Syria at a food stall in the magnificent ancient souk of Aleppo. The secret lay in the combination of slow-roasted sweet red peppers and walnuts with fresh pomegranate molasses. While you could buy jarred roasted peppers, it's far tastier—and not at all difficult—to roast fresh red peppers yourself. This savory dip, with its coarse texture and spicy, sweet-sour taste, offers a delightful alternative to hummus.

SERVES 4

3 tablespoons extra-virgin olive oil, divided
2 red bell peppers, seeded and roughly chopped
2 tablespoons sweet red pepper paste
1 garlic clove, peeled
1 tablespoon pomegranate molasses
1 tablespoon Aleppo pepper or chili flakes
1 tablespoon lemon juice
½ cup (2 ½ oz/75 g) pomegranate seeds, plus more for garnish
¾ cup (2 ½ oz/75 g) walnuts, toasted and roughly chopped, plus more for garnish
1 teaspoon sesame seeds, for garnish
1 green onion, finely chopped, for garnish (optional)
Flatbread, crackers, or romaine lettuce leaves, for serving

In a medium nonstick pan over low heat, warm 2 tablespoons of the olive oil and cook the chopped peppers until soft and the skin blisters or chars, about 20 minutes.

In a blender or food processor, combine the cooked peppers, pepper paste, garlic, pomegranate molasses, Aleppo pepper, lemon juice, and remaining 1 tablespoon olive oil and purée for 3 minutes. Spoon the purée into a bowl or onto a plate and cool for 15 minutes.

Stir the pomegranate seeds and walnuts into the purée with a spoon.

Garnish the muhammara with additional pomegranate seeds, walnuts, sesame seeds, and if desired, green onion. Serve at room temperature with flatbread, crackers, or wrapped in a lettuce leaf.

Yarqunto di lhana *cabbage salad*
with roasted almonds

My mother prepares this cabbage salad with dried mint, sesame seeds, garlic, paprika, olive oil, and lemon juice. She always makes a large bowl because nobody can get enough of it. Roasted almonds are not traditionally included, however, my mother contends that they enhance the flavor and texture.

SERVES 6

1 pound (500 g) green cabbage, grated
3 tablespoons dried mint
1 tablespoon sesame seeds, toasted
1 tablespoon garlic powder
2 teaspoons paprika
5 tablespoons extra-virgin olive oil
Juice of ½ lemon
Salt and freshly ground pepper
1 cup (3 ½ oz/100 g) almonds, toasted and roughly chopped

In a large bowl, combine the cabbage, mint, sesame seeds, garlic powder, paprika, olive oil, and lemon juice. Toss to combine. Add salt and pepper to taste. Sprinkle the salad with toasted almonds and serve immediately.

Yarqunto fattoush *toasted bread salad*

One of the most popular salads among the Assyrians, and indeed almost all peoples in the Middle East, is yarqunto fattoush. It's delicious and a great way to use leftover bread. The base of the salad is vegetables and herbs that are readily available, and the salad is then topped with pieces of bread toasted to perfection and added at the last moment to preserve their satisfying crunch. Traditional yarqunto fattoush varies with the seasons depending on what is growing in the garden.

SERVES 6

For the dressing:
¼ cup (2 fl oz/50 ml) extra-virgin olive oil
2 tablespoons pomegranate molasses
Juice of 1 lemon
1 garlic clove, finely chopped
3 teaspoons salt

For the salad:
1 head romaine lettuce, coarsely chopped
1 cup (1 oz/30 g) summer purslane, stems removed, or arugula
2 small cucumbers, coarsely chopped into cubes
3 tomatoes, coarsely chopped into cubes
5 radishes, thinly sliced
3 green onions, sliced into rings
1 bell pepper, seeded and coarsely chopped into cubes
5 ½ ounces of pomegranate seeds
2 teaspoons sumac
1 tablespoon dried mint
Leaves from ½ bunch fresh mint, coarsely chopped
Leaves from ½ bunch flat-leaf parsley, coarsely chopped
1 tablespoon sunflower oil
2 flatbreads

Make the dressing: In a mixing bowl, whisk together the olive oil, pomegranate molasses, lemon juice, garlic, and salt.

Make the salad: In a large bowl, combine the lettuce, purslane, cucumbers, tomatoes, radishes, green onions, bell peppers, pomegranate seeds, sumac, dried and fresh mint, and parsley. Stir in the dressing and toss to combine. Taste and adjust seasoning with salt as necessary. Let the salad sit for about 15 minutes.

In a large skillet over medium heat, warm the sunflower oil and toast the flatbreads on both sides until crispy. Turn off the heat and tear the bread into small pieces.

Stir the crispy bread pieces into the salad and serve immediately.

Ballo' *spicy appetizer of red lentils and bulgur*

Ballo', an Assyrian finger food, is one of the oldest dishes in this cookbook. However, it also aligns with modern culinary trends as it is a spicy, 100% vegan snack. Ballo' is made from finely ground bulgur and cooked red lentils (which are actually orange in color), and was originally made during fasting periods or when there was no meat available. Today, it is enjoyed as an appetizer on festive occasions and is easily made in large quantities.

MAKES 18 PIECES

For the lentils:
2 ½ cups (600 ml) cold water
1 cup (7 oz/200 g) red lentils
2 teaspoons sunflower oil
4 teaspoons salt, divided
1 ½ cups (9 oz/250 g) fine-grain bulgur
1 teaspoon tomato paste
1 teaspoon ground coriander
1 teaspoon paprika
2 teaspoons extra-virgin olive oil
1 teaspoon freshly ground pepper
½ cup (120 ml) warm water
2 green onions, thinly sliced
1 tablespoon sambal (Indonesian chile paste)
Juice of ½ lemon
¼ bunch flat-leaf parsley, finely chopped
Baby romaine leaves, for serving (optional)
Raw vegetables (radishes, green onions, turnips), for serving (optional)

In a deep pot over medium heat, bring the water, lentils, sunflower oil, and 2 teaspoons of the salt to a boil. Reduce the heat to low and simmer for 15 minutes, stirring occasionally and skimming off any rising foam with a spoon.

In a large bowl, combine the bulgur, tomato paste, coriander, paprika, olive oil, pepper, and the remaining 2 teaspoons of salt. Carefully pour the warm lentils into the bowl and stir everything together. Let the mixture cool for 30 minutes in a dry, draft-free place.

Pour the warm water into the mixture and knead the dough until it's smooth and cohesive. If the mixture seems dry or isn't coming together well, adjust by adding more warm water or olive oil as needed. Add the green onions, sambal, lemon juice, and parsley, combining everything well.

With your hands, shape the mixture into 18 balls, then press each ball into an oval shape, about 3 inches (8 cm) in length.

Serve at room temperature, ideally with a leaf of romaine lettuce to pick up each snack and raw vegetables on the side.

Faṣuliye ḥeworo *white bean casserole*

In the village of Sare, where my mother grew up, people cultivated grains, fruits, and vegetables, and also legumes such as chickpeas, lentils, and white beans. The summer harvest was typically abundant, providing more than enough produce for winter. My mother would string some of the harvest into chains to hang and dry, including various vegetables like tomatoes and eggplants. During the cold winter months, a brief soak in hot water would rejuvenate them, making them seem "fresh" again. The dried white beans used in this recipe are store-bought and don't have holes from threading, but the result is no less delicious, especially when served with warm vermicelli rice.

SERVES 8

3 cups (650 g) dried white beans
2 tablespoons sunflower oil
6 ½ cups (1.5 l) water
4 tablespoons tomato paste
1 teaspoon sambal (Indonesian chile paste)
1 teaspoon paprika
1 teaspoon lemon juice
1 tablespoon salt
1 teaspoon freshly ground pepper
A handful of coarsely chopped flat-leaf parsley
Vermicelli rice (pg. 49), for serving

Place the white beans in a large deep pot and add cold water to cover the beans by several inches. Let them soak for 2 hours and then drain. Dry out the pot.

In the same pot over low heat, warm the sunflower oil and sauté the white beans for 10 minutes over low heat, stirring well to prevent them from sticking to the bottom or burning.

Add the water and bring to a boil. Stir in the tomato paste, sambal, paprika, lemon juice, and salt and pepper. Lower the heat, cover the pot, and let the beans simmer for about 90 minutes, adding extra water if necessary, until they are soft and tender but still hold their shape. Adjust seasoning with salt and pepper if needed.

Sprinkle the beans with parsley and serve warm with a side of vermicelli rice.

BAṢRONÉ U NUNÉ

──────── Meat and Fish

Tawayee di patata - Acin - Basro 'al dawqo - Be'e da dayroye - Gyothe melye - Gyothe mqalye - Gyothe shliqe - Kebab - Bacanat komé hashye - Nuno zafaran - Nuné shliqe

Smuni Turan, *my mother.*

Soon after my parents were married, their first child was born. Several years later, they relocated to Istanbul for of a promising job opportunity for my father. The allure of the metropolis was too great for my mother to resist. It transformed her life dramatically.

"My daughter was just six months old when we journeyed to Istanbul. For three days and nights, we traveled together by train. My husband had gone ahead of us, having secured a good job. My brother lived there as well, along with three of my husband's brothers. We all shared a home. We had no oven, but we could take our casserole to the baker's oven. Using the baker's oven was a common practice; everyone in the neighborhood did so. A whole new world opened up to me. I had never seen a banana, much less eaten one. The same goes for cauliflower and broccoli. And of course, cola! I had never tasted it before! At first, it tasted too intense, but soon, I couldn't get enough of it. And all the new sweet things, like Turkish delight, were enticing."

"We had no oven, but we could take our casserole to the baker's oven."

"Then there were the shop windows. Beautiful clothes, pantsuits, nail polish, lipstick—I was unfamiliar with all of these things. Istanbul introduced me to modern life. We had more money, we dined out at restaurants, and I bought beautiful clothes, handbags, and shoes. I was young and discovering a whole new life. My mother cried the first time she saw me wearing high heels and flared trousers, which were the fashion at the time. But they were tears of joy—joy for my beautiful life and the bright future that lay ahead. Soon after, my eldest son was born."

Read more on page 184

Tawayee di patata *one-pan dish with potatoes, tomatoes, and ground meat*

The tawa, a cast-iron pan or casserole dish, can be used either in the oven or on the stove. See the dish of the same name on page 67. If cooked on the stovetop, the dish is called *tawayee*, which roughly means "a pan that is pleasingly full." For her version of it, I remember my mother would alternate endless layers of tomato, lemon, and potato with aromatic herbs and ground meat. The allure of this dish lies in the juices released at the bottom, which are perfect for dipping bread into. Tawayee is a one-pot dish and once it's on the stove, it doesn't require your attention for an hour. For us as kids, the waiting was quite a trial. "Hands off!" my mother would say sternly if one of us dared to lift the lid.

SERVES 4

1 teaspoon unsalted butter, melted
1 pound (500 g) lean ground beef
1 white onion, chopped
2 garlic cloves, minced
1 teaspoon paprika
1 tablespoon tomato paste
2 teaspoons chili flakes
2 teaspoons allspice
½ bunch flat-leaf parsley, coarsely chopped
3 teaspoons salt
2 teaspoons freshly ground pepper
6 waxy potatoes, peeled and thinly sliced
7 vine tomatoes, thinly sliced
½ lemon, thinly sliced
2 tablespoons (30 ml) water
1 teaspoon chili flakes, for garnish
¼ bunch flat-leaf parsley, finely chopped, for garnish
Crusty bread or steamed rice, for serving

Special equipment: a straight-sided frying pan with a lid, approximately 11 inches (28 cm) in diameter and 2 ½ inches (6 cm) deep

Grease the pan with the butter. In a large bowl, combine the ground beef, onion, garlic, paprika, tomato paste, chili flakes, allspice, parsley, and salt and pepper. Mix well, and press the ground meat mixture evenly and firmly into the bottom of the pan.

Arrange the potato slices and half the tomato slices in two alternating layers over the meat. Next, create a third layer with the lemon slices and the remaining tomato slices. Pour the water into the pan and cover with a lid.

Transfer the pan to the stove and cook over high heat for approximately 5 minutes. Then, reduce the heat to low and let everything simmer for 55 minutes, until the beef is cooked through and the vegetables are tender.

Remove the lid and sprinkle the dish with chili flakes and parsley. Serve warm, with bread or rice.

Acin *steak tartare, Assyrian style*

The French have their steak tartare, but in our cuisine, we have a dish called acin (pronounced "aadjzien"). It's made from lean, ultra-fresh beef or lamb mixed with extra-fine bulgur and seasoned with salt, pepper, and spices. The bulgur lends a delicate texture and acts as a binding agent, imparting a refined taste to the dish. We consume it in a less refined way, however; we eat acin with a rolled-up romaine lettuce leaf straight from the plate, no knife or fork needed. My mother also likes to top it with a sunny-side-up egg, making it a perfect main course.

SERVES 10

- 1 white onion, finely chopped
- ½ teaspoon salt
- 1 ½ cups (9 ounces or 250 g) extra-fine-grain bulgur
- 4 tablespoons extra-virgin olive oil
- 1 tablespoon paprika
- ½ tablespoon ground cumin
- 1 tablespoon ground coriander
- ½ tablespoon freshly ground pepper
- ⅔ cup (5 fl oz/150 ml) cold water, divided
- 2 tablespoons hot pepper paste
- 1 teaspoon dried mint
- 2 cups (18 oz/500 g) high quality raw beef or lamb tartare, freshly prepared
- 1 bunch flat-leaf parsley, finely chopped
- 30 pitted black olives (such as Kalamata)

Special equipment: a mortar and pestle

Place the onion and salt in a mortar (or food processor) and grind to a fine texture. In a large bowl, combine the onion mixture with the bulgur and olive oil. Mix the ingredients well until all oil is absorbed. Add the paprika, cumin, coriander, pepper, and about two-thirds of the cold water. Mix again, incorporating the water until it is absorbed. Add the pepper paste and mint, then knead again. Add the raw beef or lamb tartare and mix thoroughly until everything is well combined.

Taste the mixture and adjust seasoning with additional salt or spices as necessary. Pour the remaining cold water into the bowl. Then mix the mixture for 20 minutes until it becomes smooth.

Evenly divide the tartare among 10 small plates and flatten each portion with a spoon. Use the tines of a fork to create a decorative pattern around the edges of the tartare. Garnish each serving generously with parsley and olives, and serve.

Basro 'al dawqo *spiced meat on mini flatbread*

When my nephews and nieces visit from abroad, they all want basro 'al dawqo. The name literally means "meat on bread." Ground meat is mixed with vegetables, spices, and herbs and then sandwiched between two layers of bread dough. It is delicious with iceberg lettuce, mint, and parsley on top. She always makes a large stack, as the whole family loves it—much like their love for Grandma, of course.

SERVES 13

For the dough:
3 ½ cups (18 oz/500 g) bread flour, plus more for dusting
2 tablespoons extra-virgin olive oil, divided
1 teaspoon salt
1 cup (8 ounces) warm water

For the meat filling:
1 ¼ cups (11 oz/300 g) ground beef
2 tablespoons tomato paste
2 tablespoons seven-spice powder
1 tablespoon paprika
1 teaspoon sambal (Indonesian chile paste)
2 teaspoons salt
1 teaspoon freshly ground pepper
2 yellow onions, finely chopped
2 vine tomatoes, seeded and finely chopped
1 green pepper, finely chopped
½ bunch flat-leaf parsley, finely chopped, plus more for serving
1 tablespoon extra-virgin olive oil

A green salad, for serving
Lemon wedges, for serving

Preheat the oven to 465°F (240°C) and line two baking sheets with parchment paper.

Make the dough: In a large bowl, combine the flour, 1 tablespoon of the olive oil, and the salt and water. Knead with your hands until the flour is absorbed. Use the remaining 1 tablespoon of olive oil to lightly grease your hands and shape the dough into a ball. If the dough is too dry, add more warm water; if it's too wet, add more flour. It's right when it doesn't stick to your hands. Divide the dough into 13 equal-sized balls, each approximately the size of a small orange, and let them rest, covered, for 15 minutes.

Make the meat filling: In a large bowl, combine the ground beef, tomato paste, seven-spice powder, paprika, sambal, and salt and pepper in a large bowl. Mix well with a spoon. Add the onions, tomatoes, green pepper, parsley, and olive oil, and knead everything by hand to combine well.

Form the basro 'al dawqo: Lightly dust your work surface with flour. Take a ball of dough and roll it out into a thin round sheet. Spread about 1 ½ tablespoons of the meat filling on the dough, leaving a border around the edges to prevent overflowing. Place the dough on the baking sheet and bake until golden brown, about 8 to 9 minutes. Repeat as necessary until all are baked.

Serve with a green salad, fresh parsley, and lemon wedges.

Be'e da dayroye *fried eggs with beef sausage*

The cuisines of the Middle East have many similarities, but that of the Assyrians is different in one major aspect: the use of alcohol. We like to enjoy a good glass of beer or wine with our meals, and raki, liqueur, and whiskey with our digestifs. Of course, we try to drink in moderation, although sometimes, when the morning after is challenging, I realize I should have passed on that last glass of raki. On those occasions, I always make be'e da dayroye—a delightful egg dish that completely perks you up, especially because of the sucuk (pronounced "suu-djuuk"), a semi-dry beef sausage with the strong, spicy flavor of garlic, pul biber (Aleppo pepper), cumin, and paprika. The egg yolk stays runny, making it perfect for dipping bread—preferably straight from the pan, as was the custom in our home.

SERVES 2

- 2 tablespoons extra-virgin olive oil
- 2 green chile peppers, seeded and sliced into half-circles
- 4 medium vine tomatoes, quartered
- 10 thin slices sucuk (or other garlic sausage)
- 4 large eggs
- 1 teaspoon paprika
- 2 teaspoons salt
- 1 teaspoon freshly ground pepper
- 1 handful coarsely chopped flat-leaf parsley, for garnish
- 1 tablespoon sesame seeds, for garnish
- 2 spring onions, white part only, sliced into thin rings, for garnish
- Warm bread, for serving

In a large nonstick skillet over medium-high heat, warm the oil and sauté the green peppers and tomatoes for 7 minutes, stirring regularly.

Spread the slices of sucuk evenly in the pan and sauté for another 2 minutes.

Crack the eggs into the pan and reduce the heat to low. Sprinkle everything with the paprika, salt, and pepper. Allow the eggs to cook about 8 minutes, until the whites are set but the yolks are still runny.

Garnish the dish with the parsley, sesame seeds, and spring onions. Serve the dish straight from the pan, with warm bread on the side for dipping.

Gyothe melye *roasted stuffed chicken with rice and vegetables*

The technique of stuffing dishes has been practiced since Mesopotamian times, when vegetables and leaves were stuffed with all kinds of delicacies. The wealthy even filled sheep, lambs, or parts thereof. My mother tried preparing meat dishes in this traditional manner for us a few times, but frankly, it was not to our liking. "Preferably chicken, mom," we would say cautiously. Fortunately, she took our preferences to heart. Her crispy roasted *gyothe melye* ("stuffed chicken") is unmatched in flavor and texture.

SERVES 5

For the stuffing:
2 tablespoons unsalted butter, divided
6 ounces (175 g) ground beef
1 teaspoon paprika
3 teaspoons salt
1 teaspoon freshly ground pepper
1 small white onion, finely chopped
1 red chile pepper, seeded and finely chopped
1 green chile pepper, seeded and finely chopped
1 red bell pepper, finely chopped
½ carrot, finely chopped
4 garlic cloves, finely chopped
½ cup (125 g) arborio rice, rinsed
1 cup (225 ml) water
¼ cup (1 oz/30 g) pine nuts, toasted
½ bunch flat-leaf parsley, coarsely chopped
1 green onion, cut into thin rings

For the chicken:
1 tablespoon lemon juice
1 tablespoon extra-virgin olive oil
1 tablespoon honey
1 tablespoon seven-spice powder or chicken spice
2 teaspoons tomato paste
1 whole chicken, about 4 pounds (1 ½–2 kg)
1 ½ cups (300 ml) water

Special equipment: a metal skewer, kitchen twine

Make the stuffing: In a Dutch oven or other deep heavy pot over medium-high heat, melt 1 tablespoon of the butter and fry the ground beef, stirring, until crumbly, approximately 4 minutes. Add the paprika, salt, and pepper, and sauté for another minute. Then add the onion and fry for 1 additional minute. Add the red chile pepper, green chile pepper, red bell pepper, carrot, garlic, rice, and the remaining 1 tablespoon of butter, and mix well. Stir continuously for 5 minutes until all the rice grains are coated. Continue to stir while adding 1 ½ cups water or enough to cover the mixture and simmer, covered, for about 20 minutes over low heat, until all the water has been absorbed by the rice.

Remove the pot from the heat. Stir the pine nuts, parsley, and green onion into the rice mixture.

Preheat the oven to 400°F (200°C).

In a medium bowl, make a marinade by whisking together the lemon juice, olive oil, honey, seven-spice powder, and tomato paste. Set aside.

Remove any innards from the chicken cavity, then fill the cavity and neck with the rice mixture. Tie the chicken legs together with twine and bind the neck with the skewer to keep the stuffing inside during cooking.

Place the chicken in a roasting pan and rub it all over with the marinade. Pour in the water. Cover the roasting pan with aluminum foil, place it in the oven, and roast the chicken for 90 minutes. Remove the pan from the oven and remove the foil. Baste the chicken with the cooking juices and return the pan to the oven for another 30 minutes. The chicken is done when the skin is golden brown and crispy, and the internal temperature reaches 165°F (74°C).

Kebab *spiced ground meat*

Who isn't familiar with a kebab sandwich served with garlic sauce and a fresh salad? However, few people know that kebab is one of the oldest dishes in the world. The word, which means "roasted meat," comes from Akkadian (*kebabu*) and was mentioned as early as 2000 BCE on clay tablets inscribed in cuneiform. The Assyrians later adopted the word and the dish. This classic, which uses ground meat, is still a favorite throughout the Middle East and, indeed, the whole world.

MAKES 10–12 KEBABS

9 ounces (250 g) ground lamb
9 ounces (250 g) ground veal
½ white onion, finely chopped
4 garlic cloves, finely chopped
2 tablespoons finely chopped parsley
1 tablespoon tomato paste
1 tablespoon Aleppo pepper
1 teaspoon paprika
1 teaspoon salt
½ teaspoon freshly ground pepper
¼ cup (1 oz/30 g) pine nuts, toasted, for garnish
Flatbread, for serving
Cucumber salad (pg. 46) for serving

In a large bowl, combine the ground lamb, veal, onion, garlic, parsley, tomato paste, Aleppo pepper, paprika, and salt and pepper, and mix well by hand.

Preheat the oven to 400°F (200°C) and line a baking sheet with parchment paper.

With damp hands, divide the ground meat into equal portions of 2 to 2 ½ ounces (60–70 g). Form each portion into a compact, firm cylinder that is long and flat, being careful not to tear the meat—this may take some practice. Keep your hands damp during the shaping.

Arrange the kebabs evenly on the baking sheet and bake for about 15 minutes or until they are golden brown and cooked through.

Remove the kebabs from the oven and sprinkle them with the toasted pine nuts. Serve with flatbread and cucumber salad.

Gyothe shliqe *braised chicken with bulgur and onion*

The secret to this dish lies in simultaneously cooking the gyothe (chicken) and bulgur in one pot, which imparts a rich and full-bodied flavor to the bulgur. When my mother was growing up, she and her grandmother would find any chicken wandering about in the yard, and would butcher it themselves. I buy mine in the store, and because a whole chicken takes much longer to cook than individual parts, I tend to use drumsticks or thighs, since I prefer a quicker cooking time for such a delicious dish.

SERVES 4

8 chicken drumsticks
1 tablespoon salt
½ tablespoon ground turmeric
½ tablespoon allspice
½ tablespoon ground ginger
½ tablespoon freshly ground pepper
½ tablespoon paprika
Juice of ½ lemon
4 tablespoons (50 g) unsalted butter
1 ½ cups (9 oz/250 g) medium-grain bulgur
1 tablespoon spicy chile paste
3 cups (700 ml) warm water
1 tablespoon extra-virgin olive oil
1 white onion, thinly sliced
2 garlic cloves, finely chopped
Leaves from ½ bunch mint, roughly chopped, for garnish
Leaves from ½ bunch flat-leaf parsley, roughly chopped, for garnish

Place the drumsticks in a Dutch oven or other heavy deep pot and add enough water to completely cover them. Add salt and bring to a boil over medium heat. Boil for 10 minutes and then drain the water and remove the chicken to a plate.

In a small bowl, combine the turmeric, allspice, ginger, pepper, paprika, and lemon juice. Mix well to make a marinade, and rub it thoroughly onto the chicken pieces. In the same Dutch oven or heavy pot over medium heat, melt the butter to the pot and then add the marinated chicken and brown it for 10 minutes, turning once halfway through. Add the bulgur, spicy chile paste, and warm water to the pot. Bring to a simmer, cover the pot, and cook for 25 minutes.

While chicken and bulgur cook, in a medium nonstick skillet over medium heat, warm the olive oil and sauté the sliced onions, stirring frequently, for 10 minutes. Add the garlic and sauté for 1 more minute.

Check to make sure the bulgur has absorbed all the liquid and that the chicken is cooked through. Remove the pot from the heat, and stir the onion mixture into the chicken and bulgur. Add salt and pepper to taste.

Transfer the mixture to a serving platter, and sprinkle with the mint and parsley.

Gyothe mqalye *spicy chicken and paprika stir-fry with sumac*

Juggling the roles of raising seven children—including cleaning, washing, ironing, grocery shopping, and cooking—is not an easy task, especially when my mother initially had only a minimal understanding of the Dutch language. But she managed, and every day, a delicious dish graced our table. "How did you manage all that, Mom?" is a question that we, like millions of other children, undoubtedly asked our mothers at some point. My mother couldn't provide an answer; somehow, she just did it, aided by quick-cooking dishes like this spicy stir-fry.

SERVES 5

5 tablespoons unsalted butter, divided
1 pound (500 g) chicken breast, cut into cubes
2 teaspoons cinnamon
2 teaspoons turmeric
2 teaspoons ground cumin
2 teaspoons salt
1 white onion, thinly sliced
2 red bell peppers, seeded and sliced into strips
1 red chile pepper, seeded and finely chopped
3 garlic cloves, finely chopped
2 tablespoons sumac
2 tablespoons pine nuts, toasted
5 tablespoons plain yogurt
1 tablespoon dried mint
Rice or bulgur, for serving
Yarqunto di lhana (cabbage salad, pg. 142), for serving

In a small pot over medium heat, melt 3 tablespoons of the butter. In a large bowl, combine the chicken, melted butter, and the cinnamon, turmeric, cumin, and salt. Cover the bowl and refrigerate for 60 minutes.

In a large skillet over medium heat, melt the remaining 2 tablespoons of butter and sauté the onion, bell peppers, and red chile peppers for 10 minutes or until softened. Turn off the heat, transfer the mixture to a plate, and set aside.

In the same skillet, sauté the chicken cubes over medium heat for 5 minutes or until cooked through. Add the garlic and sumac and sauté for 1 more minute.

Return the onion-pepper mixture to the pan and stir-fry everything for 1 more minute. Sprinkle the toasted pine nuts over the top.

In a small bowl, stir together the yogurt and the dried mint. Serve the stir-fry with a dollop of the yogurt, with rice or bulgur and a cabbage salad (pg. 142) on the side.

Bacanat komé hashye *stuffed eggplants with ground beef*

The Assyrian call eggplants *bacanat komé*, "black tomatoes." Yet there's no other vegetable in our cuisine that we cook with more. We fry them, puree them, pickle them, and roast them in the oven. Bacanat komé hashye (stuffed eggplants) is my favorite eggplant recipe, not just because of the mildly sweet, sharp taste, but also because they look so festive.

SERVES 5

- 5 medium eggplants
- 4 tablespoons extra-virgin olive oil, divided
- 3 garlic cloves, finely chopped
- ½ pound (200 g) lean ground beef
- 2 white onions, coarsely chopped
- 1 green chile pepper, seeded and finely chopped
- 1 tablespoon seven-spice powder
- 1 tablespoon chili powder
- 2 teaspoons paprika
- 2 teaspoons salt
- 2 teaspoons freshly ground pepper
- 3 tablespoons tomato paste
- 1 cup (200 ml) water
- 3 tablespoons lemon juice
- Lemon slices (optional)
- 1 ½ cups (9 oz/250 g) sweet cherry tomatoes, on the vine
- 5 sprigs flat-leaf parsley, roughly chopped

Preheat the oven to 425°F (220°C) and line a baking sheet with parchment paper.

Slice the eggplants lengthwise, but do not cut all the way through. Use your fingers to scoop out approximately half of the flesh, and set it aside in a bowl. Lightly brush the outside of the eggplant with 1 tablespoon total of the olive oil and place them on the prepared baking sheet. Bake for 25 minutes. Remove from oven and set aside; keep the oven on.

While eggplants cook, in a medium nonstick pan over medium heat, warm 1 tablespoon of the olive oil and add the garlic and the reserved eggplant flesh. Sauté for 5 minutes or until tender. Set the mixture aside.

In a large skillet over high heat, warm the remaining 2 tablespoons of olive oil and cook the ground beef, breaking it up with a spoon, for 4 minutes. Add the onion, green pepper, seven-spice powder, chili powder, paprika, and salt and pepper. Stir well and sauté for approximately 5 minutes, until the onions are translucent. Mix in the sautéed eggplant flesh and continue to cook for another 2 minutes.

In a roasting pan or other oven-safe dish, lay the eggplants next to each other and stuff them with the beef mixture.

In a measuring cup, mix the tomato paste, water, and lemon juice, add salt and pepper to taste, and pour this mixture over the eggplants. If desired, add additional garlic or fresh lemon slices to the dish for extra flavor. Cover the dish with aluminum foil and place it in the oven for 25 minutes.

Remove the foil and scatter the cherry tomatoes over the eggplants, pressing them in. Bake, uncovered, for an additional 20 minutes.

Remove the dish from the oven and spoon any liquid at the bottom over the eggplants. Sprinkle with parsley and serve.

Nuno zafaran *whitefish with saffron, mint, dill, and peas*

The Dyrul Zafaran monastery is located in the Tur Abdin region, the area where my parents grew up. It is one of the world's oldest Christian monasteries. Built in 493 CE on the remnants of a solar temple over four thousand years old, it offers religious instruction and Aramaic language lessons to this day. Dyrul Zafaran is also known as the Saffron Monastery, a name reflecting the warm yellow hue of the building's stones. The mortar is rumored to have been laced with saffron during construction. Whenever my mother prepares nuno zafaran, a dish of fish with saffron, this monastery comes to mind. She uses this precious spice sparingly due to its costliness. While many Middle Eastern stores sell acceptable substitutes, the authentic saffron, of course, tastes the best. It requires only a small amount to give a dish its refined flavor and color.

SERVES 6

2 cups (10 ½ oz/300 g) frozen peas
boiling water (enough to cover the peas)
1 cup (250 ml) fish stock
1 ½ pinches (30 threads) saffron
6 (6-oz/170g) fillets whitefish, like cod, branzino, or dorade
Salt and freshly ground pepper
⅔ cup (150 ml) heavy cream, at room temperature
½ bunch mint leaves, coarsely chopped
½ bunch dill, finely chopped
Cooked rice, for serving

Preheat the oven to 350°F (180°C).

Place the frozen peas in a pot and cover them with boiling water. Let them sit for 3 minutes, and then drain.

In a small saucepan over low heat, simmer the fish stock until reduced to about ⅔ cup (150 ml). Add the saffron and stir for 2 minutes or until it is fully steeped. Turn off the heat and set the pot aside.

Generously season both sides of the fish fillets with salt and pepper and place them in an oven dish. Transfer the dish to the oven and bake for 15 minutes or until fish is cooked through.

While the fish cooks, prepare the sauce: Warm up the reduced saffron fish stock over medium heat. Reduce the heat to low and add heavy cream, peas, mint, and dill, stirring for 2 minutes. Be careful not to let the sauce boil.

Turn off the heat and season the sauce with salt and pepper to taste.

Remove the fish from the oven and pour the sauce over it. Serve with rice.

Nuné shliqe *fish cooked in white wine with lentils*

In Sare, the Christian village in present-day Eastern Turkey where my mother grew up, fish was rarely eaten. She recalls an uncle occasionally bringing pickled swordfish, but nothing beyond that. Nevertheless, my mother now prepares delicious fish dishes that she's learned from relatives living nearer to the sea or a river. This recipe features fish cooked in white wine and served with a delectable lentil salad. I usually opt for cod, but any whitefish will do. Pair it with a glass of white wine for the perfect finishing touch!

SERVES 4

1 cup (6 oz/170 g) dried green lentils, rinsed
2 ½ cups (625 ml) water, divided
Juice of 1 lemon
1 pound (400 g) cod
4 tablespoons pomegranate molasses
2 tablespoons extra-virgin olive oil
3 vine tomatoes, finely chopped
½ cup (2 ½ oz/70 g) pitted green olives, sliced
¼ cup (1 oz/25 g) pine nuts, toasted
3 green onions, white part only, thinly sliced
½ bunch cilantro, coarsely chopped
½ cup (125 ml) dry white wine
1 teaspoon salt
1 teaspoon freshly ground pepper

In a medium pot over medium heat, bring the lentils and 2 cups of the water to a boil. Cover the pot and simmer on low heat for 20 minutes or until tender.

While lentils cook, pour the lemon juice onto a plate and dip both sides of the cod into the juice. Set the fish aside on a plate or piece of aluminum foil.

Transfer the cooked lentils to a large bowl. Add the pomegranate molasses, olive oil, tomatoes, olives, pine nuts, green onions, and cilantro, and mix to combine. Add salt and pepper to taste.

In a wide pan, bring the wine and remaining ½ cup water to a boil. Add 1 teaspoon each of salt and pepper. Add the cod, reduce the heat to low, and let it simmer for 10 minutes, until cooked through.

Carefully remove the fish from the pan to a plate. Use a fork or your hands to flake it into pieces. Season with salt and pepper to taste. Mix the warm fish pieces into the lentil salad, and serve immediately.

ḤALYUTHO

Divine Sweets

Seble ~ 'Oliqé ~ Baqlawa ~ Dashisto ~ Harise ~ Kleicha ~
Lahmo halyo ~ Gabula ~ Raha doe debis da hinwe ~ Qawité

Smuni Turan, *my mother.*

In the early 1970s, my mother relocated with her family to the Netherlands. It was a challenging time, marked by profound homesickness. Her struggles were magnified by the language barrier and the unfamiliar customs.

"My husband got a new job in the Netherlands, and I stayed in Istanbul with our two children while we figured out the logistics of the relocation. Once a year, my husband would visit during the summer holiday. Throughout the year, he would send letters, money, and gifts. After three years, on October 28, 1973, I followed him to the Netherlands. Once there, I found that produce such as eggplant, zucchini, and bell peppers were scarce or, at times, unavailable. Occasionally I could find them at Turkish stores, but they (especially eggplant) cost a hefty price. This eventually changed, but for several years, our diet mainly consisted of overcooked, mushy potatoes, which were unpleasant. I had to learn a new way of cooking. Now, my children eat everything, except sheep, lamb, or stuffed tripe. This preference has always seemed a bit unfortunate to me."

"Aside from two other families, my husband and I were the first Assyrians in the Netherlands. We settled in Hengelo, where my husband founded a church. Initially, we attended a regular Catholic church. But as our community grew, it was time to build our own church. Everyone contributed money, and my husband led the fundraising and construction efforts. The church was a great success, and even a Syriac Orthodox monastery was added in Glane. My husband also served as a contact person for other Assyrians who wished to move to the Netherlands. He handled the paperwork and also arranged for safe houses, as some came illegally. Sometimes we had up to twenty-five people staying in our house at one time.

"I cooked for all these people. They couldn't afford to pay; they were political refugees."

"They had to register at the town hall to apply for asylum. I cooked for all these people. They couldn't afford to pay; they were political refugees. They carried only a suitcase with some clothes—that was all. In their homeland, they were tortured and persecuted for being Christians. The first person we accommodated was my husband's brother. Then, my two brothers arrived as well.

"The success in managing to secure legal status for everyone drew attention and made people wonder how Smuni and Garibo could achieve this. More and more people came to us. We even received letters from an American priest in the United States, urging us to take people in and assist them. Occasionally, the immigration police would visit, asserting that we were harboring individuals without the proper permits. I would deny it outright. Hiding people wasn't easy, especially as the police would sometimes conduct thorough searches of the entire house. Once, during a search, I hid a young man behind the curtain of the crib where Matay was lying. He and the children that followed were all born in the Netherlands. In total, I had seven children."

Read on the page 213

Seble *crumble cake with walnuts, coconut, and apricot jam*

I wouldn't be surprised if *seble*, the name of one of my favorite cakes, originates from the French word *sable*, meaning "sand." The presence of the French in the region where my mother grew up—parts of Syria, Lebanon, and Southeast Turkey—undeniably left its culinary mark. Seble is a shortbread cake with a crunchy crumble texture, but it's not dry, thanks to the addition of apricot jam and coconut. It's from the Middle East, yet imbued with a hint of French elegance.

SERVES 10

4 large eggs
1 ½ cups (345 g) unsalted butter, melted plus more for greasing
1 tablespoon vanilla extract
½ cup (100 g) granulated sugar
Grated zest of 1 lemon
3 teaspoons baking powder
6 ½ cups (750 g) all-purpose flour, divided
½ cup (130 g) apricot jam
1 cup (100 g) coarsely chopped walnuts
¼ cup (25 g) ground coconut, plus more for sprinkling

Special equipment: a 13-inch (33-cm) round baking tin

In a large bowl, use a hand mixer to mix the eggs, butter, vanilla extract, granulated sugar, and lemon zest for 5 minutes. Sift in the baking powder and ⅓ of the flour. Then, knead the mixture together by hand. Sift in ½ of the remaining flour and knead again. Add the rest of the flour and knead until a smooth dough forms. The dough should not feel sticky.

Divide the dough into two equal portions. Put one portion in a freezer bag and place it in the freezer for 15 minutes.

Preheat the oven to 365°F (185°C). Grease the base and walls of the baking tin with melted butter.

Spread one portion of the dough over the base of the baking tin and press gently into an even layer. Spread the apricot jam evenly over the dough. Sprinkle the chopped walnuts and coconut over the jam.

Remove the dough from the freezer and use a coarse grater to grate the dough over the walnut-jam filling. Continue until the walnuts are no longer visible. (You may not use all the dough; any leftover portion can be used to bake small cookies.)

Place the baking tin in the middle of the oven and bake the cake until light brown, about 40–45 minutes. Remove the tin from the oven and sprinkle with extra ground coconut. Allow the cake to cool completely in the tin.

Cut the cake into slices and, if desired, serve with additional apricot jam and walnuts. Store any leftovers in the fridge for up to 2 days, and in the freezer for up to 7 days.

Raha doe debis da hinwe *caramelized pistachio-orange bar with grape molasses*

Despite the multitude of candy bars and energy bars available on the market, I find myself continually drawn to a simple, traditional treat my mother used to make during our childhood: raha doe debis da hinwe. The words essentially translate to "candy made of grape molasses," which is the foundation of this irresistible delicacy. It is a perfect snack, suitable with coffee, tea, or at any time.

MAKES 12 BARS

½ cup (3 ½ oz/100 g) superfine sugar
2 tablespoons boiling water
1 tablespoon unsalted butter
1 tablespoon lemon juice
½ teaspoon salt
¼ cup (2 oz/50 g) grape molasses or light molasses
Zest of ½ orange
½ cup (3 ½ oz/100 g) raw pumpkin seeds
1 cup (5 ½ oz/150 g) shelled, unsalted pistachios, divided

Cover a large, flat plate or round baking tin with parchment paper.

In a deep pot with a thick bottom, mix together the sugar, water, butter, lemon juice, and salt. Bring the mixture to a boil over medium heat, and stir continuously with a whisk for 1–2 minutes.

Reduce the heat to low, add the molasses, and let the mixture simmer for 10 minutes, stirring occasionally.

Remove the pan from the heat and, using a spoon, stir in the orange zest, pumpkin seeds, and half the pistachios.

Quickly transfer the mixture from the pan to the prepared plate. Sprinkle the remaining pistachios evenly on top, and cover with another sheet of parchment paper. Press down firmly with your hands to create a round slab about ½ inch thick. Place the plate in the refrigerator and let it set for about 60 minutes.

Once the slab is set, cut into bars. If they feel sticky, dust the bars with a little cornstarch or powdered sugar. Store them in the refrigerator (they tend to soften at room temperature).

Harise *semolina cake with almond and orange*

In my mother's village, there were neither bakeries nor pastry chefs. Everything was made at home. If a sweet smell was wafting from the oven, it was often harise—a dish that's somewhere between a cake and a tart, made of fine semolina from hard wheat. Harise is baked in a round springform pan soaked in sugar syrup, cut into squares, and finally sprinkled with sliced almonds. The syrup, known as atter, is the star. Combined with the airy cake, it is simply irresistible. Atter is also used to make lemonade, usually with reduced fruits, but there are also variations with herbs and even flowers.

SERVES 10

4 large eggs
2 tablespoons lemon juice, divided
2 ¼ cups (16 oz/450 g) sugar
1 ¼ cups (275 ml) sunflower oil
1 ⅓ cups (300 ml) plain yogurt
3 ½ cups (18 oz/500 g) semolina
Zest of 1 orange
5 tablespoons (32 g) baking powder
2 cups (450 ml) water
½ cup (2 ½ oz/75 g) sliced almonds

Special equipment: a 14 ½-inch (37-cm) round springform pan, greased

Preheat the oven to 350°F (175°C).

In a large bowl, whisk together the eggs, 1 tablespoon of the lemon juice, and the oil. Add the yogurt, semolina, and orange zest, and beat until the mixture is light and airy. Let it rest for 20 minutes. Add the baking powder and mix until everything is well combined.

In a saucepan over low heat, bring the water, remaining 3 cups sugar, and remaining 1 tablespoon lemon juice to a simmer. Let it simmer very gently for 45 minutes, stirring regularly, until the sugar has dissolved.

Pour the batter into the cake mold and smooth the top. Sprinkle the sliced almonds over it in an even layer. Bake the cake in the oven for 30–35 minutes, until golden brown.

While still in the pan, cut the cake into square or rectangular pieces. Gradually pour the hot sugar syrup over the warm cake. Let the cake cool for 30 minutes before serving.

Gabula *warm wheat with dried plums and ground melon seeds*

Ground melon seeds? I must admit, I was also surprised when my mother told me about this breakfast dish from her childhood. It's called gabula, and its distinctive flavor comes from a part usually discarded: the melon seeds. Instead of tossing them away, my mother preserved them: drying, roasting, grinding them in a mill, and then sieving them into a powder. Intrigued, I decided to try it immediately, simply because I had never seen this use before. And the result is truly astounding; seldom have I tasted a dish with such a refined, nutty flavor.

SERVES 4

5 ½ cups (1 ⅓ l) water
1 ⅓ cups (9 oz/250 g) coarse wheat groats
1 tablespoon salt
1 teaspoon extra-virgin olive oil
3 ½ ounces (100 g) dried cantaloupe melon seeds
½ cup plain yogurt, for topping
20 dried pitted plums, for topping
Honey, for topping

Special equipment: a coffee grinder or spice grinder

In a large pot over high heat, bring the water to a boil. Add the wheat groats and salt and stir continuously, using a spoon to skim off any foam that rises to the top. After 15 minutes, reduce the heat to low, add the olive oil, and simmer for an additional 20 minutes or until the groats are tender and the mixture has thickened.

In a small skillet over low heat, toast the melon seeds, shaking regularly to prevent burning, just until the seeds start to turn golden. Let the seeds cool, then transfer them to a coffee or spice grinder and grind until they are a fine powder. Shake the powder through a sieve into a bowl. Discard any pieces left in the sieve.

Serve the warm wheat in deep bowls. Top with yogurt, the melon seed powder, and dried plums. Add honey to taste.

Lahmo halyo *soft sweet rolls*

The Assyrian observe a fast not only in the days preceding Easter but also for ten days before Christmas. Twice a year, a joyous occasion ensues when the fasting period ends, and the unique sweet scent of lahmo halyo wafts from the oven in the morning. The bread is also known as chorek, which translates to "kneaded" (in Greece, it is called tsoureki), and this kneading is undertaken with much care and affection. The outcome is a soft, sweet bread reminiscent of French brioche. Upon returning from church, a breakfast table laden with butter, jam, white cheese, eggs, and black tea awaited us, and we would be especially eager for the round or braided rolls. My mother always served herself last, waiting to see our approval of the rolls. The age-old tradition holds that lahmo halyo must be perfect. If it's not, then the festivities are marred. This gives an almost sacred status to the bread. One ingredient can never be absent: mastic (pg. 28), a spice derived from the mastic tree with a flavor somewhere between wood and fresh pine. However, we children never thought much about tradition; we simply couldn't get enough of the bread.

MAKES APPROX. 35 ROLLS

¾ cup (200 ml) plus 1 teaspoon whole milk, divided
¾ cup (180 g) granulated sugar
2 sticks plus 2 tablespoons (1 cup or 250 g) unsalted butter
2 ¼ teaspoons active dry yeast (¼ oz/ 7 g) or ¾ ounce (20 g) fresh yeast
½ cup (100 ml) water
8 cups (1 kg) wheat flour
4 teaspoons (16 g) vanilla extract
4 teaspoons (16 g) baking powder
1 heaping tablespoon finely ground mahlab
1 heaping tablespoon nigella seeds
1 teaspoon finely ground mastic
4 large eggs
1 tablespoon sunflower oil
2 egg yolks

In a small saucepan over low heat, gently warm the ¾ cup of milk and the sugar (do not let the milk boil). Stir continuously until the sugar has dissolved.

In another small saucepan, melt the butter over low heat.

In a small bowl, stir together the yeast and water and set aside.

In a large mixing bowl, stir together the flour, vanilla extract, baking powder, mahlab, nigella seeds, and mastic. Add the yeast mixture and knead by hand into a smooth dough. Add the 4 whole eggs and knead thoroughly for about 5 minutes. Pour in the milk-sugar mixture and knead again. Pour the melted butter into the bottom of the bowl (not over the dough) and knead for 10 minutes more. Add the sunflower oil and knead everything for 1 more minute until a smooth and pliable dough ball is formed.

Cover the bowl containing the dough ball with a dry tea towel (and perhaps a thick coat for added insulation, as my mother always does) and let it rise in a draft-free place for 90 minutes, until it has doubled in volume.

Preheat the oven to 400°F (200°C). Line two baking sheets with parchment paper. In a small bowl, whisk together the egg yolks and the remaining 1 teaspoon milk.

Roll the dough between your palms into about 35 balls. Flatten each ball into a circle (about 3 ½ inches or 9 cm in diameter) using your palm. Place the dough circles on the lined baking sheet, ¾ inch (2 cm) apart.

Brush the dough circles with the egg yolk mixture. Bake the rolls for 20–25 minutes, until golden brown. Allow them to cool on a wire rack. Serve within a day, or wrap and freeze them for up to 2 months.

TIP

If you want to create a large braided bread instead of rolls, divide the dough into 3 equal dough strands. Place them next to each other, pinch the ends together on one side, and alternately weave the left and right strands over the middle one. Continue this way until you reach the bottom of the strands, pinching the ends together at the bottom. Bake for approximately 35 minutes or until the bread is toasty brown in color.

Kleicha *light and crunchy spice cookies*

Of all the recipes in this cookbook, this is undoubtedly one of the oldest. It is known that thousands of years ago in Mesopotamia, dough was sweetened with fruit or spiced with seasonings. The word *kleicha* comes from the term *ko laysho*, which means "she makes dough" (*laysho* translates to "dough"). It is my favorite childhood cookie. These cookies are enjoyed especially during Easter and Christmas, when people bake them in vast quantities. They're not only favorites among the Assyrians, but also enjoy widespread popularity throughout the Middle East. Of course, there are a hundred and one variations. All families have their own recipes, each varying in spices and their proportions, depending on the family's ancestral origins. My mother has her own recipe, which I still find (of course) the most delicious.

MAKES 32 COOKIES

½ cup (100 ml) water
½ cup (90 g) granulated sugar
1 ½ sticks (170 g) unsalted butter
2 teaspoons (8 g) baking powder
2 teaspoons (8 g) vanilla extract
1 tablespoon ground mahlab
2 tablespoons nigella seeds
1 ½ teaspoons ground cinnamon
1 teaspoon ground aniseed
½ teaspoon ground cloves
½ teaspoon ground cardamom
½ teaspoon ground allspice
½ teaspoon ground nutmeg
4 cups (500 g) wheat flour
1 teaspoon (4 g) instant yeast or 1 ½ teaspoons active dry yeast
2 large eggs, separated
¼ cup (50 ml) sunflower oil
1 tablespoon milk or lemon juice

In a small saucepan over low heat, warm the water and sugar (do not let boil), stirring until the sugar is dissolved. Remove from the heat.

In another small saucepan over low heat, melt the butter. Remove from the heat and let cool to lukewarm before using.

In a large bowl, combine the baking powder, vanilla extract, mahlab, nigella seeds, cinnamon, aniseed, cloves, cardamom, allspice, and nutmeg. Sift the flour through a fine sieve into the bowl. Add the sugar water, the yeast, and the egg whites, and knead for about 4 minutes. Add the melted butter and knead by hand until fully incorporated. Add the sunflower oil and continue to knead by hand for 15 minutes until the mixture forms a smooth dough. Form into a ball, cover the bowl with a dry kitchen towel, and allow the dough to rise in a draft-free area for 60 minutes or until it slightly increases in volume.

Line two baking sheets with parchment paper.

Roll the dough between your palms into 32 balls. Flatten each ball into a circle (about 1 ¼ inches or 3 cm in diameter) using your palm. Place the dough circles on the lined baking sheet, 1 inch (2 cm) apart. Let the dough rest at room temperature for 20 minutes.

While the dough rests, preheat the oven to 425°F (220°C). In a small bowl, whisk together the egg yolks and the milk or lemon juice.

Brush the tops and sides of the dough with the egg yolk mixture. Bake the cookies for 10–12 minutes, until golden brown. Remove the baking sheet from the oven and let the cookies cool for 10 minutes, then move them to a wire rack. Serve them immediately, or store them for up to 4 days in an airtight container at room temperature. They can also be frozen for later use.

Baqlawa (or baklava) *phyllo pastry filled with walnuts*

The sweet aroma of baqlawa can be found wafting through the streets of any city in the Middle East. The origins of baqlawa are not entirely clear, but a plausible theory suggests that the Assyrians, my ancestors, were the first to bake layers of bread with walnuts in between around 800 BCE. The term baqlawa directly translates to "layers." There are countless variations, flavors, textures, shapes, and colors, but of course, my mother makes the best. Her Assyrian version is uniquely characterized by its simplicity. It focuses on essential ingredients like butter, sugar, and coarsely ground walnuts while omitting raisins, rose water, and honey. Those who taste it must have strong willpower to stop at just one piece.

MAKES 30–40 PIECES

2 ½ cups (10 ½ oz/300 g) walnuts
1 teaspoon ground cinnamon
1 pound (470 g) phyllo dough, thawed
4 sticks (2 cups/500 g) unsalted butter
⅔ cup (140 g) granulated sugar
¼ cup (70 g) water
¼ teaspoon fresh orange juice

Special equipment: a rectangular oven dish or baking mold (approximately 12 x 16 x 1.6 inches/30 x 40 x 4 cm)

Preheat the oven to 350°F (180°C).

Place the walnuts and cinnamon in a food processor and grind to a medium-coarse texture, being careful not to turn it into flour. Measure out 5 tablespoons of the mixture and set aside.

Trim the phyllo sheets to fit the baking dish by placing the dish over the dough and trimming around it. Try to avoid leaving the dough out of the package for too long, as it will dry out.

In a medium saucepan, melt the butter. Spoon off the white milk solids, leaving just the clear yellow liquid (clarified butter).

Brush the bottom and sides of the baking dish with the clarified butter, then evenly cover the bottom with the scraps of phyllo you trimmed off earlier. Brush this "scraps layer" with 2 tablespoons of melted butter and cover with a sheet of phyllo dough. Continue this process, brushing each sheet with 2 tablespoons of melted butter. Repeat until you have 8 total layers. To keep the baqlawa light and airy, do not press down on the sheets.

Spread the walnut filling from the food processor over the top sheet. Place a new sheet over the filling, brush with melted butter, and repeat the process as needed until all filling is used up. Finish with the remaining sheets, brushing each sheet with the melted butter.

Using a sharp knife, cut the baqlawa into diamond or square pieces, making sure to cut through the bottom layer. Pour the remaining melted butter over the baqlawa and bake for 30 minutes, or until golden brown and cooked through.

While the baqlawa bakes, in a small saucepan over medium heat, combine the sugar, water, and orange juice in a pan and bring to a boil, stirring well until the sugar has dissolved. Reduce the heat to low to keep the syrup warm.
Remove the baqlawa from the oven, pour the warm sugar syrup over it, and sprinkle with the remaining 5 tablespoons of ground walnuts.

TIP

Turkish stores often sell fresh, large sheets of phyllo dough for making baqlawa, providing a superior alternative to the frozen phyllo dough available at supermarkets.

Dashisto *sweet rice pudding*

This simple rice pudding, enjoyed warm or cold, is a favorite during Easter. Everyone looks forward to dashisto after the Lent period, during which no dairy is consumed. Its aroma of warm milk and sugar is irresistible.

My mother once told me that dashisto was also distributed to conclude the forty-day mourning period following the death of a loved one, making it comfort food in the most literal sense of the word. Sometimes the pudding was replaced by lentil soup (pg. 96), but only if the fortieth day fell within a fasting period. In such cases, all animal products, including milk, were avoided.

SERVES 4

¼ cup (50 ml) water
1 cup (7 oz/200 g) arborio rice, rinsed
3 cups (750 ml) whole milk
¼ cup (50 g) granulated sugar
1 teaspoon ground cinnamon
2 fresh figs, diced
1/4 cup roasted pistachios

In a deep saucepan over medium heat, bring the water to a boil and add the rice. Stir well and let it cook for about 4 minutes.

Pour the milk into the pan, add the sugar, and stir, bringing it to a simmer. Reduce the heat to very low and let it simmer gently for about 25 minutes, making sure it doesn't boil. Keep stirring until the rice is cooked through but still firm. If the pudding appears dry, gradually add more milk or water. Remove from heat and let the pudding cool for 2 minutes.

Spoon the pudding onto 4 plates, and sprinkle with the cinnamon, diced figs, and pistachios. Alternatively, skip the toppings and let the pudding cool (it can be served cold, at room temperature, or warm).

'Oliqé *walnut strings in grape molasses*

'Oliqé (pronounced "olikee") likely takes its name from the term *eloqo*, which translates to "hang" or "suspend." 'Oliqé are strings of walnuts threaded on a long wire and immersed in hot grape molasses. They are left to dry outdoors on a rope or branch. The technique is somewhat akin to the making of dip candles. My mother used to prepare the molasses herself, a concoction of condensed grape juice, but now we simply purchase the molasses in a jar. I still find the unique flavor of 'oliqé spectacular. Slightly bittersweet with a robust bite—no energy bar can match it!

MAKES 8 WALNUT STRINGS

160 walnut halves (20 walnut halves per string)
4 cups (950 ml) water
2 cups (500 ml) grape molasses or light molasses
⅔ cup (150 g) all-purpose flour

Special equipment:
a thin, sharp needle
6 ½ feet (2 meters) of thin, sturdy cotton thread
clothespins

Cut the thread into 8 equal pieces. Thread one piece through the eye of the needle and tie a knot at the end of the thread. Pierce the needle through the middle of 20 walnut halves, then tie a knot at the other end to secure them. The string with the walnuts attached should measure around 8–10 inches (20-25 cm). Repeat this process with the other pieces of thread and the remaining walnuts.

In a deep pot over high heat, bring the water to a boil. Whisk in the grape molasses until smooth. Add the flour and mix thoroughly, stirring for approximately 5 minutes until the flour is fully incorporated. Remove from heat and strain the mixture through a sieve into a bowl to remove lumps. Transfer the contents of the bowl back to the pot and cook over low heat, stirring, for a few minutes until it becomes thick and syrupy. Remove from heat.

Holding a walnut string by the top, lower the threaded walnuts into the mixture. Use a spoon as necessary to spread the mixture and ensure that all sides of the walnuts are evenly coated. Immediately hang the walnut string with a clothespin on a clothesline or loop it over a stick suspended horizontally. Repeat this process with the remaining walnut strings, and let them dry at room temperature for a minimum of 3 days. As the juice dries, the molasses coating will harden.

Qawité — Ninive's pick-me-up cake

The Assyrians observe more fasting periods than many other faith communities. In particular, the Saumo Ninive (pg. 19) is a stringent fast, spanning three days without food or drink. I'll be frank—my mother and I would prefer to opt out of the fasting and just indulge in the traditional reward after such a time of deprivation: qawité, a cake of grape molasses packed with everything needed to regain strength. The word *qawité* is derived from the word *quwa*, meaning "strength" or "pick-me-up." This traditional dish, dating back thousands of years, was originally made from grape molasses and seven kinds of grains from the land. Today, the grains have been partly supplemented with chickpeas, nuts, seeds, and kernels, all roasted and finely ground. Originally, Galia melon seeds were used, but pumpkin seeds work just as well.

SERVES 6

- 3 ½ ounces (100 g) fine wheat semolina
- 2 tablespoons (1 oz/25 g) fine corn semolina
- 2 tablespoons (1 oz/25 g) wheat flour
- 2 tablespoons (1 oz/25 g) dried chickpeas
- 2 tablespoons (1 oz/25 g) sesame seeds
- 2 tablespoons (1 oz/25 g) almonds
- 2 ounces (50 g) walnuts
- 3 ounces (75 g) Galia melon seeds or pumpkin seeds
- ¼ teaspoon ground cinnamon
- 1 ¾ cups (400 ml) boiling water
- 1 ½ cups (300 ml) grape molasses or light molasses
- ½ teaspoon salt
- grapes, for garnish
- nuts, for garnish

In 8 bowls or small dishes, place the following ingredients: wheat semolina, corn semolina, flour, chickpeas, sesame seeds, almonds, walnuts, and melon seeds. In a dry pan, toast each ingredient one by one over medium heat, being careful to avoid burning. Return each toasted ingredient to its bowl to cool.

In a food processor or coffee grinder, separately grind the chickpeas, sesame seeds, almonds, walnuts, and melon seeds.

In a large bowl, combine all the ground ingredients except the melon seeds. Add the wheat semolina, corn semolina, flour, and cinnamon and mix well. Sift the mixture into another large bowl, shaking the sieve gently. Separately, sift the ground melon seeds into the bowl, discarding any remaining fragments from the sieve.

In a large pot over high heat, bring the water, grape molasses, and salt to a boil, stirring. Add the mixture of ground ingredients and stir until well blended. Remove the pot from heat and let cool for 2 hours.

Transfer the contents of the pot to a bowl. Wet your hands and knead the dough for a few minutes. It should be firm yet soft. Transfer the dough to a plate and use your hands to shape it into a smooth, round cake. Garnish the qawité with nuts and grapes.

Smuni Turan, *my mother.*

Even after living in the Netherlands for such a long time, my mother still has a lingering sense of nostalgia for her homeland.

"I returned to my birth village once, in 2007. My brother and nephew had rebuilt and renovated our ancestral home. My parents' land is a grape paradise. We made raisins. We enjoyed delightful meals at a restaurant overlooking the border with Syria. We savored wine from the vintner Shiluh, who maintains the tradition of producing Assyrian wine. This wine tradition is centuries old and is said to have originated in Mesopotamia."

> ## "We savored wine from the vintner Shiluh, who maintains the tradition of producing Assyrian wine."

"Yet, I was also very saddened: most of the houses in our village were destroyed, and hardly anyone lived there anymore. The majority of people had been driven away, most Christians had left, and much of the culture had consequently been lost. They've become ghost towns. The house where I lived with my husband was still there. At the church, we encountered the mayor, who greeted us. He remembered my husband. We also visited a few centuries-old monasteries. The priest was angry because many Christians had emigrated, however, one might wonder what alternatives exist in such circumstances. Living there during that time was unbearable and simply dangerous."

Although some families have returned in recent years, most Assyrian villages in the region are still deserted.

Acknowledgments: *Taudi sagi!*

Virtually all dishes and ingredients in this book have been given their original Aramaic or Assyrian names, along with their English translations. One ingredient I have forgotten: *taudi sagi*—in our language, it means "many thanks!" Because, to be honest, without the help of many talented people, no dish would have found its way onto any of the pages of this book.

First and foremost, the biggest taudi sagi goes to my mother. As I have written elsewhere, she is, in fact, the author of this book. All the recipes were in her head; I just had to listen to her and watch how she worked in her kitchen. At the same time, I listened to the stories of her youth, her origin, her culture. Cooking and good conversations just go well together. It provided a fascinating insight into a way of life that hardly exists anymore. Next, a huge taudi sagi for the enthusiasm of Ronit Palache, who immediately embraced the idea of this cookbook and found the way to the publisher for me. A few more women to whom I want to express taudi sagi with warm feelings: my sisters Yildez, Susan, and Linda who brainstormed and read along ("you didn't forget the samborakat, did you?"), my sister Jacqueline, who helped with styling ("Mom, sit still for the makeup"), photographer Emma Peijnenburg ("can that lamp be turned off? I want only natural light"), photographer and visual artist Claire Witteveen ("not again with the parsley and lemons!"), and designer Marjolein Meulendijks ("I think Cormorant Garamond with serifs is the most beautiful").

And then the men. First of all, my good friend Daan Heijbroek, who took the photo that encapsulates the entire book in one image: the recipes passed down from a mother to her children. It was immediately clear that this should be the cover photo. I also want to thank photographer Milan Gino, who, with great patience, got my sister and her children Violette, Céline, and Jack in front of the camera. Then Rany Elyo, my cousin, who helped me with the correct translations from Surayt, Suret(h), and Akkadian. Finally, I also thank my dear friend Romke Oortwijn for his refreshing contributions to the text. As I write this acknowledgment, I suddenly realize that this book has largely come together through people who have not been part of making a cookbook before. No food stylists or photographers were involved. But, of course, without professionals, there is no book. I thank Francis Wehkamp, Willemijn Visser, Milou Breunesse, and Marije Braat from Fontaine Publishers, who know better than anyone what they are doing. The same goes for Nigel Slater and Karin Hamersma, who read the manuscript and wrote kind words about it. So, two kind words back: taudi sagi!

Index

A

Aleppo pepper:
Kebab (spiced ground meat) 168
Muhammara (spicy roasted pepper dip with pomegranate) 139
Qar'ukkat (scrambled eggs with zucchini and garlic) 118
Yarqunto semaqto (roasted red cabbage with feta, mint, and pistachios) 121

Almonds:
Harise (semolina cake with almond and orange) 191
Qawité (Ninive's pick-me-up cake) 208
Yarqunto di lhana (cabbage salad with roasted almonds) 142

Aniseed:
Kleicha (light and crunchy spice cookies) 199
Apprakhe (stuffed grape leaves) 70
Yarqunto (simple Assyrian vegetable salad) 56
Atter (simple sugar syrup) 191

Appetizers:
Ballo' (spicy appetizers with red lentils and bulgur) 146
Be'e da dayroye (fried eggs with beef sausage) 162
Gyothe melye (roasted stuffed chicken with rice and vegetables) 165
Muhammara (spicy roasted pepper dip with pomegranate) 139
Nuné shliqe (fish cooked in white wine with lentils) 181
Tlawhé (traditional red lentil soup) 96
Yarqunto fattoush (toasted bread salad) 145
Yarqunto semaqto (roasted red cabbage with feta, mint, and pistachios) 121

Yarqunto tabouleh (tabouleh parsley salad) 122

Apricot jam:
Seble (crumble cake with walnuts, coconut, and apricot jam) 187

B

Bacanat komé hashye (stuffed eggplants with ground beef) 175
Ballo' (spicy appetizers of red lentils and bulgur) 146
Bamya (okra stew with beef) 103
Baqlawa (phyllo pastry filled with walnuts) 200
Basle hashye (braised stuffed onions) 77

Basmati rice:
Mujadarah (lentils and rice with caramelized onions) 131
Basro 'al dawqo (spiced minced meat on mini flatbread) 159
Be'e da dayroye (fried eggs with beef sausage) 162

Beans, white:
Fasuliye heworo (white bean casserole) 149

Beef, ground:
Apprakhe (stuffed grape leaves) 70
Bacanat komé hashye (stuffed eggplants with ground beef) 175
Basle hashye (braised stuffed onions) 77
Basro 'al dawqo (spiced minced meat on mini flatbread) 159
Gyothe melye (roasted stuffed chicken with rice and vegetables) 165
Kibbeh seniye (baked bulgur and ground meat pie) 74
Kötle (stuffed wheat pouches) 80
Maqloubeh (upside-down savory pie) 88
M'wothé (meat and grain sausage) 90

Samborakat (crescent moons of stuffed dough) 64
Tawa (casserole with meat and vegetables) 67
Tawayee di patata (one pan dish with potato, tomato, and meat) 155

Beef stew:
Bamya (okra stew with beef) 103
Marga (spicy onion beef stew) 109

Beef tartare:
Acin (steak tartare, Assyrian style) 156

Beef sausage:
Be'e da dayroye (fried eggs with beef sausage) 162

Beets, red:
Yarqunto da saldemee (beet salad with chickpeas) 135

Bell peppers:
Fulful hashyo (stuffed bell peppers) 73
Gyothe mqalye (spicy chicken and paprika stir-fry with sumac) 172
Hemse (chickpea soup) 100
Itj (bulgur balls) 125
Makdous (stuffed baby eggplants) 132
Marga (spicy onion beef stew) 109
Muhammara (spicy roasted pepper dip with pomegranate) 139
Yarqunto fattoush (toasted bread salad) 145

Bread:
Basro 'al dawqo (spiced minced meat on mini flatbread) 159
Dawqo hamiğe (pan-baked flatbread) 55
Lahmo doe tanuro (clay oven bread) 84

Lahmo halyo (soft sweet rolls) 196
Yarqunto fattoush (toasted bread salad) 145

Bulgur:
Ballo' (spicy appetizers with red lentils and bulgur) 146
Bulgur (with fried onions) 42
Bulgur (with vermicelli) 42
Itj (bulgur balls) 125
Gyothe shliqe (braised chicken with bulgur and onions) 171
Kibbeh seniye (baked bulgur and meat pie) 74
Kötle (stuffed wheat pouches) 80
M'wothé (meat and grain sausage) 90

C

Cabbage, red:
Yarqunto semaqto (roasted red cabbage with feta, mint, and pistachios) 121

Cabbage, white:
Yarqunto di lhana (cabbage salad with roasted almonds) 142

Cake:
Harise (semolina cake with almond and orange) 191
Qawité (Ninive's pick-me-up cake) 208
Seble (crumble cake with walnuts, coconut, and apricot jam) 187

Carrot:
Tlawhé (traditional red lentil soup) 96
Gyothe melye (roasted stuffed chicken with rice and vegetables) 165

Cheese:
Gweto (white raw-milk cheese) 52
Yarqunto semaqto (roasted red cabbage with feta, mint, and pistachios) 121

Cherry tomatoes:
Bacanat komé hashye (stuffed eggplants with ground beef) 175
Kebab (spiced ground meat) 168

Cod:
Nuné shliqe (fish cooked in white wine with lentils) 181

Chile pepper:
Apprakhe (stuffed grape leaves) 70
Bacanat komé hashye (stuffed eggplants with ground beef) 175
Be'e da dayroye (fried eggs with beef sausage) 162
Fulful hashyo (stuffed bell peppers) 73
Gerso (warm and creamy wheat) 99
Gyothe melye (roasted stuffed chicken with rice and vegetables) 165
Kebab (spiced ground meat) 168
Muhammara (spicy roasted pepper dip with pomegranate) 139
Nuné shliqe (fish cooked in white wine with lentils) 181
Qar'ukkat (scrambled eggs with zucchini and garlic) 118
Tawayee di patata (one pan dish with potato, tomato, and meat) 155
Tlawhé (traditional red lentil soup) 96
Yarqunto semaqto (roasted red cabbage with feta, mint, and pistachios) 121

Cilantro:
Bamya (okra stew with beef) 103
Gyothe shliqe (braised chicken with bulgur and onions) 171
Qar'ukkat (scrambled eggs with zucchini and garlic) 118
Tlawhé (traditional red lentil soup) 96
Yarqunto fattoush (toasted bread salad) 145
Yarqunto tabouleh (tabouleh parsley salad) 122

Cinnamon:
Atayef (stuffed pancakes with nuts) 198
Ballo' (spicy appetizers of red lentils and bulgur) 146
Basro 'al dawqo (spiced minced meat on mini flatbread) 159

Gyothe melye (roasted stuffed chicken with rice and vegetables) 165
Harise (semolina cake with almond and orange) 191
Kleicha (light and crunchy spice cookies) 199
Lahmo halyo (soft sweet rolls) 196
Maqloubeh (upside-down savory pie) 88
Muhammara (spicy roasted pepper dip with pomegranate) 139
Seble (crumble cake with walnuts, coconut, and apricot jam) 187
Tlawhé (traditional red lentil soup) 96
Yarqunto di lhana (cabbage salad with roasted almonds) 142

Chicken:
Gyothe melye (roasted stuffed chicken with rice and vegetables) 165
Gyothe mqalye (spicy chicken and paprika stir-fry with sumac) 172
Gyothe shliqe (braised chicken with bulgur and onions) 171

Chickpeas:
Hemse (chickpea soup) 100
Hemse thine (creamy hummus with tahini) 126
Yarqunto da saldemee (beet salad with chickpeas) 135

Cookies:
Kleicha (light and crunchy spice cookies) 199

Coconut:
Seble (crumble cake with walnuts, coconut, and apricot jam) 187

Cologne 36

Cream:
Gerso (warm and creamy wheat) 99
Maqloubeh (upside-down savory pie) 88
Muhammara (spicy roasted pepper dip with pomegranate) 139

Seble (crumble cake with walnuts, coconut, and apricot jam) 187
Crushed tomatoes:
Tawayee di patata (one pan dish with potato, tomato, and meat) 155

Cucumber:
Khase da bosine (refreshing yogurt cucumber salad with dill) 46
Yarqunto (simple Assyrian vegetable salad) 56
Yarqunto fattoush (toasted bread salad) 145

Cumin:
Be'e da dayroye (fried eggs with beef sausage) 162
Fulful hashyo (stuffed bell peppers) 73
Gyothe shliqe (braised chicken with bulgur and onions) 171
Muhammara (spicy roasted pepper dip with pomegranate) 139
Nuné shliqe (fish cooked in white wine with lentils) 181

D

Dried mint:
Ballo' (spicy appetizers of red lentils and bulgur) 146
Gyothe melye (roasted stuffed chicken with rice and vegetables) 165
Khase da bosine (refreshing yogurt cucumber salad with dill) 46
Yarqunto fattoush (toasted bread salad) 145
Yarqunto semaqto (roasted red cabbage with feta, mint, and pistachios) 121
Yarqunto di Lhana (cabbage salad with roasted almonds) 142

E

eggs:
Be'e da dayroye (fried eggs with beef sausage) 162
Basro 'al dawqo (spiced minced meat on mini flatbread) 159
Gyothe melye (roasted stuffed chicken with rice and vegetables) 165

Lahmo doe tanuro (clay oven bread) 84
Nuné shliqe (fish cooked in white wine with lentils) 181
Qar'ukkat (scrambled eggs with zucchini and garlic) 118
Seble (crumble cake with walnuts, coconut, and apricot jam) 187
Tawayee di patata (one pan dish with potato, tomato, and meat) 155
Twayyo semaqto (lentil salad with roasted red cabbage) 105
Twayyo shliqe (lentil salad with cooked chicken) 104

Eggs, red:
Be'é semoqe (natural red eggs) 136

Eggplant:
Bacanat komé hashye (stuffed eggplants with ground beef) 175
Fasuliye heworo (white bean casserole) 149
Makdous (stuffed baby eggplants) 132
Maqloubeh (upside-down savory pie) 88
Tawa (casserole with meat and vegetables) 67

F

Feta cheese:
Yarqunto fattoush (toasted bread salad) 145
Yarqunto semaqto (roasted red cabbage with feta, mint, and pistachios) 121

Figs:
Dashisto (sweet rice pudding) 204
Yarqunto da saldemee (beet salad with chickpeas) 135

Fish:
Nuné shliqe (fish cooked in white wine with lentils) 181
Nuno zafaran (whitefish with saffron, mint, dill, and peas) 178

Flatbread:
Basro 'al dawqo (spiced minced meat on mini flatbread) 159

Dawqo hamiğe (pan-baked flatbread) 55
Lahmo doe tanuro (clay oven bread) 84
Yarqunto fattoush (toasted bread salad) 145

Fresh parsley:
Bacanat komé hashye (stuffed eggplants with ground beef) 175
Basle hashye (braised stuffed onions) 77
Basro 'al dawqo (spiced minced meat on mini flatbread) 159
Be'e da dayroye (fried eggs with beef sausage) 162
Bulgur (with fried onions or vermicelli) 42
Fasuliye heworo (white bean casserole) 149
Fulful hashyo (stuffed bell peppers) 73
Gyothe melye (roasted stuffed chicken with rice and vegetables) 165
Hemse (chickpea soup) 100
Kebab (spiced ground meat) 168
Kötle (stuffed wheat pouches) 80
Samborakat (crescent moons of stuffed dough) 64
Tawa (casserole with meat and vegetables) 67
Tawayee di patata (one pan dish with potato, tomato, and meat) 155
Yarqunto tabouleh (tabouleh parsley salad) 122
Yarqunto fattoush (toasted bread salad) 145

Fried eggs:
Be'e da dayroye (fried eggs with beef sausage) 162

G

Gabula (warm wheat with dried plums and ground melon seeds) 194
Gerso (warm and creamy wheat) 99

Grape leaves:
Apprakhe (stuffed grape leaves) 70

Green beans:
Matfuniye fasuliye yaroqo (green bean and lamb stew) 110

Green onions:
Ballo' (spicy appetizers of red lentils and bulgur) 146

Green pepper:
Bulgur 42
Tawa 67
Tlawhé 96
Qar'ukkat 118
Basro 'al dawqo 159
Be'e da daroya 162
Bacanat komé hashye 175

Green pepper, Turkish:
Basro 'al dawqo (spiced minced meat on mini flatbread) 159

Gweto (white raw-milk cheese) 52

Gyothe melye (roasted stuffed chicken with rice and vegetables) 165

Gyothe mqalye (spicy chicken and paprika stir-fry with sumac) 172

Gyothe shliqe (braised chicken with bulgur and onions) 171

H
Harise (semolina cake with almond and orange) 191

I
Itj (bulgur balls) 125

K
Kleicha (light and crunchy spice cookies) 199

Kötle (stuffed wheat pouches) 80

L
Labaniyeh (yogurt with hulled wheat) 83

Lahmo doe tanuro (clay oven bread) 84

Lahmo halyo (soft sweet rolls) 196

Lamb leg:
Dobo (lamb leg with garlic and spice) 106

Lamb, ground:
Apprakhe (stuffed grape leaves) 70
Kebab (spiced ground meat) 168

Lamb stew meat:
Matfuniye fasuliye yaroqo (green bean and lamb stew) 110

Lamb:
Acin (steak tartare, Assyrian style) 156

Lentils:
Ballo' (spicy appetizers of red lentils and bulgur) 146
Mujadarah (lentils and rice with caramelized onions) 131
Nuné shliqe (fish cooked in white wine with lentils) 181
Tlawhé (traditional red lentil soup) 96

Lahmo halyo (soft sweet rolls) 196

M
Makdous (stuffed baby eggplants) 132
Maqloubeh (upside-down savory pie) 88
Marga (spicy onion beef stew) 109
Matfuniye doe farmo (oven-baked zucchini stew) 113
Matfuniye fasuliye yaroqo (green bean and lamb stew) 110

Long-grain rice:
Rezo sh'iraye (vermicelli rice) 49
Tlawhé (traditional red lentil soup) 96

Mahlab:
Lahmo halyo (soft sweet rolls) 196

Mastic:
Lahmo halyo (soft sweet rolls) 196

Melon seeds:
Gabula (warm wheat with dried plums and ground melon seeds) 194
Qawité (Ninive's pick-me-up cake) 208

Mint:
Acin (steak tartare, Assyrian style) 156
Apprakhe (stuffed grape leaves) 70
Basle hashye (braised stuffed onions) 77
Basro 'al dawqo (spiced minced meat on mini flatbread) 159
Dawġe (refreshing yogurt drink) 59
Fulful hashyo (stuffed bell peppers) 73
Gyothe mqalye (spicy chicken and paprika stir-fry with sumac) 172
Khase da bosine (refreshing yogurt cucumber salad with dill) 46
Labaniyeh (yogurt with hulled wheat) 83
M'wothé (meat and grain sausage) 90
Nuno zafaran (whitefish with saffron, mint, dill, and peas) 178
Yarqunto di lhana (cabbage salad with roasted almonds) 142
Yarqunto fattoush (toasted bread salad) 145
Yarqunto semaqto (roasted red cabbage with feta, mint, and pistachios) 121
Yarqunto tabouleh (tabouleh parsley salad) 122
Muhammara (spicy roasted pepper dip with pomegranate) 139
Mujadarah (lentils and rice with caramelized onion) 131
M'wothé (meat and grain sausage) 90

N
Nigella seeds:
Kleicha (light and crunchy spice cookies) 199
Lahmo doe tanuro (clay oven bread) 84
Lahmo halyo (soft sweet rolls) 196

Nuné shliqe (fish cooked in white wine with lentils) 181

Nuno zafaran (whitefish with saffron, mint, dill, and peas) 178

O

Okra:
Bamya (okra stew with beef) 103

'Oliqé (walnut strings in grape molasses) 207

Onion, red:
Basle hashye (braised stuffed onions) 77
Itj (bulgur balls) 125
Yarqunto (simple Assyrian vegetable salad) 56

Onion, white:
Acin (steak tartare, Assyrian style) 156
Bacanat komé hashye (stuffed eggplants with ground beef) 175
Bamya (okra stew with beef) 103
Basle hashye (braised stuffed onions) 77
Basro 'al dawqo (spiced minced meat on mini flatbread) 159
Bulgur (with fried onions) 42
Be'é semoqe (natural red eggs) 136
Fulful hashyo (stuffed bell peppers) 73
Gerso (warm and creamy wheat) 99
Gyothe melye (roasted stuffed chicken with rice and vegetables) 165
Gyothe mqalye (spicy chicken and paprika stir-fry with sumac) 172
Gyothe shliqe (braised chicken with bulgur and onions) 171
Hemse (chickpea soup) 100
Kebab (spiced ground meat) 168
Kibbeh seniye (baked bulgur and meat pie) 74
Kötle (stuffed wheat pouches) 80
Maqloubeh (upside-down savory pie) 88
Marga (spicy onion beef stew) 109
Matfuniye doe farmo (oven-baked zucchini stew) 113

Matfuniye fașuliye yaroqo (green bean and lamb stew) 110
Mujadarah (lentils and rice with caramelized onion) 131
M'wothé (meat and grain sausage) 90
Samborakat (crescent moons of stuffed dough) 64
Tawa (casserole with meat and vegetables) 67
Tawayee di patata (one pan dish with potato, tomato, and meat) 155
Tlawhé (traditional red lentil soup) 96

Orange:
Harise (semolina cake with almond and orange) 191
Raha doe debis da hinwe (caramelized pistachio-orange bar with grape molasses) 188

P

Paprika:
Acin (steak tartare, Assyrian style) 156
Fulful hashyo (stuffed bell peppers) 73
Gyothe melye (roasted stuffed chicken with rice and vegetables) 165
Gyothe mqalye (spicy chicken and paprika stir-fry with sumac) 172
Gyothe shliqe (braised chicken with bulgur and onions) 171
Hemse (chickpea soup) 100
Itj (bulgur balls) 125
Kibbeh seniye (baked bulgur and meat pie) 74
Makdous (stuffed baby eggplants) 132
Marga (spicy onion beef stew) 109
Matfuniye doe farmo (oven-baked zucchini stew) 113
Muhammara (spicy roasted pepper dip with pomegranate) 139
Yarqunto fattoush (toasted bread salad) 145
Yarqunto tabouleh (tabouleh parsley salad) 122

Phyllo pastry:
Baqlawa (phyllo pastry filled with walnuts) 200

Pie, savory:
Kibbeh seniye (baked bulgur and meat pie) 74
Maqloubeh (upside-down savory pie) 88

Pine nuts:
Gyothe melye (roasted stuffed chicken with rice and vegetables) 165
Gyothe mqalye (spicy chicken and paprika stir-fry with sumac) 172
Kebab (spiced ground meat) 168
Kibbeh seniye (baked bulgur and meat pie) 74
Maqloubeh (upside-down savory pie) 88

Pistachios:
Dashisto (sweet rice pudding) 204
Raha doe debis da hinwe (caramelized pistachio-orange bar with grape molasses) 188
Yarqunto semaqto (roasted red cabbage with feta, mint, and pistachios) 121

Plums:
Gabula (warm wheat with dried plums and ground melon seeds) 194

Pomegranate molasses:
Apprakhe (stuffed grape leaves) 70
Muhammara (spicy roasted pepper dip with pomegranate) 139
Nuné shliqe (fish cooked in white wine with lentils) 181

Pomegranate seeds:
Muhammara (spicy roasted pepper dip with pomegranate) 139
Mujadarah (lentils and rice with caramelized onions) 131
Yarqunto fattoush (toasted bread salad) 145

Potato:
Tawayee di patata (one pan dish with potato, tomato, and meat) 155
Tlawhé (traditional red lentil soup) 96
Acin (steak tartare, Assyrian style) 156

Pudding:
Dashisto (sweet rice pudding) 204

Pumpkin seeds:
Raha doe debis da hinwe (caramelized pistachio-orange bar with grape molasses) 188
Qawité (Ninive's pick-me-up cake) 208

Purslane:
Yarqunto fattoush (toasted bread salad) 145

Q

Qar'ukkat (scrambled eggs with zucchini and garlic) 118

Qatiro (rich and creamy homemade yogurt) 45

Qawité (Ninive's pick-me-up cake) 208

R

Radishes:
Yarqunto fattoush (toasted bread salad) 145

Raha doe debis da hinwe (caramelized pistachio-orange bar with grape molasses) 188

Rezo sh'iraye (vermicelli rice) 49

Red beets:
Yarqunto da saldemee (beet salad with chickpeas) 135

Red lentils:
Ballo' (spicy appetizers of red lentils and bulgur) 146

Tlawhé (traditional red lentil soup) 96

Red onion:
Basle hashye (braised stuffed onions) 77
Itj (bulgur balls) 125
Yarqunto (simple Assyrian vegetable salad) 56

Red cabbage:
Yarqunto semaqto (roasted red cabbage with feta, mint, and pistachios) 121

Rice, basmati:
Mujadarah (lentils and rice with caramelized onion) 131

Rice, long-grain:
Rezo sh'iraye (vermicelli rice) 49
Tlawhé (traditional red lentil soup) 96

Rice, arborio:
Apprakhe (stuffed grape leaves) 70
Basle hashye (braised stuffed onions) 77
Dashisto (sweet rice pudding) 204
Fulful hashyo (stuffed bell peppers) 73
Gyothe melye (roasted stuffed chicken with rice and vegetables) 165
Maqloubeh (upside-down savory pie) 88
M'wothé (meat and grain sausage) 90

Roma tomatoes:
Bamya (okra stew with beef) 103
Matfuniye faṣuliye yaroqo (green bean and lamb stew) 110
Tawa (casserole with meat and vegetables) 67
Yarqunto tabouleh (tabouleh parsley salad) 122

Romaine lettuce:
Yarqunto fattoush (toasted bread salad) 145
Yarqunto tabouleh (tabouleh parsley salad) 122

S

Saffron:
Nuno zafaran (whitefish with saffron, mint, dill, and peas) 178

Salads:
Khase da bosine (refreshing yogurt cucumber salad with dill) 46
Nuné shliqe (fish cooked in white wine with lentils) 181
Yarqunto (simple Assyrian vegetable salad) 56
Yarqunto da saldemee (beet salad with chickpeas) 135
Yarqunto di lhana (cabbage salad with roasted almonds) 142
Yarqunto fattoush (toasted bread salad) 145
Yarqunto tabouleh (tabouleh parsley salad) 122

Samborakat (crescent moons of stuffed dough) 64

Seble (crumble cake with walnuts, coconut, and apricot jam) 187

Scrambled eggs:
Qar'ukkat (scrambled eggs with zucchini and garlic) 118

Semolina:
Harise (semolina cake with almond and orange) 191
Qawité (Ninive's pick-me-up cake) 208

Sesame seeds:
Be'e da dayroye (fried eggs with beef sausage) 162
Hemse (chickpea soup) 100
Muhammara (spicy roasted pepper dip with pomegranate) 139
Qawité (Ninive's pick-me-up cake) 208
Yarqunto di lhana (cabbage salad with roasted almonds) 142

Simple syrup:
Harise (semolina cake with almond and orange) 191

Soup:
Hemse (chickpea soup) 100
Tlawhé (traditional red lentil soup) 96

Sucuk:
Be'e da dayroye (fried eggs with beef sausage) 162

Sumac:
Basle hashye (braised stuffed onions) 77
Fulful hashyo (stuffed bell peppers) 73
Gyothe mqalye (spicy chicken and paprika stir-fry with sumac) 172
Yarqunto fattoush (toasted bread salad) 145

T
Tahini:
Hemse thine (creamy hummus with tahini) 126

Thyme:
Yarqunto semaqto (roasted red cabbage with feta, mint, and pistachios) 121

Tomatoes:
Apprakhe (stuffed grape leaves) 70
Bacanat komé hashye (stuffed eggplants with ground beef) 175
Bamya (okra stew with beef) 103
Basro 'al dawqo (spiced minced meat on mini flatbread) 159
Be'e da dayroye (fried eggs with beef sausage) 162
Maqloubeh (upside-down savory pie) 88
Marga (spicy onion beef stew) 109
Matfuniye doe farmo (oven-baked zucchini stew) 113
Matfuniye faṣuliye yaroqo (green bean and lamb stew) 110
Nuné shliqe (fish cooked in white wine with lentils) 181
Tawa (casserole with meat and vegetables) 67
Tawayee di patata (one pan dish with potato, tomato, and meat) 155
Yarqunto (simple Assyrian vegetable salad) 56
Yarqunto fattoush (toasted bread salad) 145
Yarqunto tabouleh (tabouleh parsley salad) 122

V
Veal minced:
Kebab (spiced ground meat) 168
Khase da bosine (refreshing yogurt cucumber salad with dill) 46
Kibbeh seniye (baked bulgur and meat pie) 74

Vermicelli:
Rezo sh'iraye (vermicelli rice) 49

W
Walnuts:
Baqlawa (phyllo pastry filled with walnuts) 200
Makdous (stuffed baby eggplants) 132
Muhammara (spicy roasted pepper dip with pomegranate) 139
'Oliqé (walnut strings in grape molasses) 207
Qawité (Ninive's pick-me-up cake) 208
Seble (crumble cake with walnuts, coconut, and apricot jam) 187
Yarqunto da saldemee (beet salad with chickpeas) 135

Wine:
Nuné shliqe (fish cooked in white wine with lentils) 181

White beans:
Fasuliye ḥeworo (white bean casserole) 149

Whitefish:
Nuno zafaran (whitefish with saffron, mint, dill, and peas) 178

Y
Yarqunto (simple Assyrian vegetable salad) 56
Yarqunto da saldemee (beet salad with chickpeas) 135
Yarqunto di lhana (cabbage salad with roasted almonds) 142
Yarqunto fattoush (toasted bread salad) 145
Yarqunto semaqto (roasted red cabbage with feta, mint, and pistachios) 121
Yarqunto tabouleh (tabouleh parsley salad) 122

Yogurt:
Dawġe (refreshing yogurt drink) 59
Gabula (warm wheat with dried plums and ground melon seeds) 194
Gyothe mqalye (spicy chicken and paprika stir-fry with sumac) 172
Harise (semolina cake with almond and orange) 191
Khase da bosine (refreshing yogurt cucumber salad with dill) 46
Labaniyeh (yogurt with hulled wheat) 83
Mujadarah (lentils and rice with caramelized onion) 131
Nuno zafaran (whitefish with saffron, mint, dill, and peas) 178
Qatiro (rich and creamy homemade yogurt) 45
Yarqunto semaqto (roasted red cabbage with feta, mint, and pistachios) 121

Copyright Page

The Oldest Kitchen in the World
4,000 Years of Middle Eastern Cooking
By Matay de Mayee

Recipes: Smuni Turan
Text: Matay de Mayee
Text Contribution: Romke Oortwijn
Photography: Emma Peijnenburg, Claire Witteveen, Daan Heijbroek
Creative Direction & Styling: Matay de Mayee
Design: Marjolein Meulendijks- Stylenoot Typesetting: Select Interface
Editing: Yulia Knol
Lithography: Pixel-it, Zutphen

U.S. Edition Publisher and Creative Director
Ilona Oppenheim

Art Director
Jefferson Quintana

U.S. Edition Cover Design
Jefferson Quintana

Designer/Typesetter
Leonardo van Schermbeek

U.S. Edition Editorial Director
Lisa McGuinness

U.S. Edition Editorial Coordinator
Jessica Faroy

Printed and bound in China
by Artron Art Co., Ltd.

The Oldest Kitchen in the World was first published in the United States by Tra Publishing, 2024.

This book was originally published as *The Oldest Kitchen in the World* by Fontaine Publishers, Amsterdam www.fontaineuitgevers.nl © 2023 Matay de Mayee.

All rights reserved. No part of this book may be reproduced or transmitted in any form or by any means (electronic or mechanical, including photocopying, recording or any information retrieval system) without permission in writing from the publisher.

ISBN: 978-1-962098-08-3

The Oldest Kitchen in the World is printed on Forest Stewardship Council®-certified paper from supporting responsible forestry.

Tra Publishing is committed to sustainability in its materials and practices.

Tra Publishing
245 NE 37th Street
Miami, FL 33137
trapublishing.com

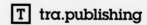

1 2 3 4 5 6 7 8 9 10